MORE FACES MORE SPACES
ARTISTS IN CANADA

MORE FACES MORE SPACES
ARTISTS IN CANADA

By Olga Dey-Bergmoser
Edited by Betty Coulter

MOSAIC PRESS
Oakville - New York - London

CANADIAN CATALOGUING IN PUBLICATION DATA

Dey-Bergmoser, Olga, 1938 -
More faces, more spaces: artists of Canada

Companion vol. to: Many faces, many spaces:
artists in Ontario.
ISBN 0-88962-487-9

1. Ethnic art - Canada. 2. Art, Canadian.
3. Art, Modern - 20th century - Canada.
I. Coulter, Betty. II. Title.

N6545.D48 1991 709'.71 C91-094056-8

This publication was supported by a grant from the Multiculturalism Directorate of the Department of the Secretary of State, Government of Canada. All views expressed here are, however, those of the author and editor.

Published by MOSAIC PRESS, P.O. Box 1032, Oakville, Ontario, L6J 5E9, Canada. Offices and warehouse at 1252 Speers Road, Units # 1 & 2, Oakville, Ontario, L6L 5N9, Canada.

Mosaic Press acknowledges the assistance of the Canada Council and the Ontario Arts Council in support of its publishing programme.

Design by Marion Black
Typeset by Jackie Ernst

Printed and bound in Hong Kong

ISBN 0-88962-467-4 CLOTH

MOSAIC PRESS:

MOSAIC PRESS, 1252 Speers Road, Units 1 & 2, Oakville, Ontario, L6L 5N9, Canada. P.O. Box 1032, Oakville, Ontario L6J 5E9

In the United States:

Distributed to the trade in the United States by: National Book Network, Inc., 4720-A Boston Way, Lanham, MD 207006 USA

In the U.K.:

John Calder (Publishers) Ltd., 9-15 Neal Street, London, WCZH9TU, England

PROLOGUE

This collection of articles portrays the passions and struggles of a sampling of Canadian artists. Here are described the years of study, concentrated effort and singleness of purpose which underlie all artistic achievement. When the creative urge is strong and is undergirded with the gift of talent, the artists have little choice but to pursue their art wherever it may lead them.

Volume I of this series, entitled: "Many Faces, Many Spaces, Artists in Ontario," was highly acclaimed as a valuable contribution to the recognition of a multicultural selection of Canadian artists.

About this book, Jill ROBINSON, Halifax book reviewer and art critic, said:

> "...What is the most interesting, is that this book deals with several artists not of a school or a generation or related in fact by any skein other than (most) being immigrants.
>
> I should find this an enlightening view about the immigrant mind and I do, a little, but - strangely - I find it more informative about me, my country, this Canada, without knowing a great deal about indigenous art and influences on visual arts in other countries. I think I see how time in Canada has now become an influence, too.
>
> One final word...with no end in sight for global village, books like this become historical documents."

"More Faces, More Spaces, Artists in Canada" is an important new book in the series which depicts a wider range of art expressions. These artists have been carefully selected from across the country. This book is also sure to win warm acceptance as an important addition to every art lover's library, for it recognizes and appreciates the diversity of talent in our midst, and the strength of the multicultural contribution to our society which enriches the lives of all of us.

CONTENTS

BETTY COULTER

Editor **Elizabeth (Betty) Joyce Coulter**
author, columnist, editor, broadcaster and creative writing instructor.

Born on a homestead to pioneering parents in the Peace River Country of Northern Alberta, this lady, who has a warm heart and contagious smile, now lives in Toronto where she is busy promoting talent in people of all ages.

Her book, TODAY, STARTING POINT FOR THE FUTURE, published recently, is a spiritual treasure chest for anyone to explore and in which to find consolation and strength.

Publ.: articles in TORONTO LIFE, THE BEAVER, 2 years series in TORONTO TELEGRAM, THE UNITED CHURCH OBSERVER and - currently - Betty also writes a column in the Etobicoke/Advertiser Guardian, a weekly community paper; is the publisher/editor of the 32,000 copy publication, THE SPIRES, a cultural community focus, and is the hostess of a cable television program, CULTURAL CRISS-CROSS.

A truly third generation Canadian with sparkling eyes full of joie de vivre, Betty is also the idealistic promoter of Canadian talent. She works with novice writers, helping them to improve their articles about people with various artistic skills, thereby encouraging all the arts. Being herself a talented writer who lives by the values she advocates, she sets an example to be emulated and shows that, although writing is usually done in solitude, one can, nevertheless, successfully lead a full family life and maintain friendships at the same time.

She believes in tight but daringly colourful writing spiced with innovative concepts and ideas - no unnecessary padding. Idealism, enthusiasm and talent alone are not enough, she feels. You need commitment, too.

Editor of Many Faces, Many Spaces
Member of the Women's Press Club of Toronto
Member of the Advisory Forum of Communication, UNICEF
Member of Arts Etobicoke
Member of the Etobicoke Social Development Council
Member of the Etobicoke Historical Society
Member of P.E.N.
Member of the Kiwanis Club of the Kingsway

OLGA DEY-BERGMOSER

Olga M. Dey-Bergmoser
Multilingual translator

Nov. 1974	-	B.A. with A-standing, U of T, Toronto
Oct. 1975	-	APUS Scholastic Award for academic excellence
Nov. 1978	-	scholarship (tuition fee refund)
Nov. 1978	-	M.A., U of T, Toronto

PUBLICATIONS: travelogues, short stories, interviews with AUTHORS and ARTISTS
December 1978 hardcover ISBN 0-919806-54-6
December 1979 paperback ISBN 0-919806-75-9
April 1981 Ltd. edition ISBN 0-919077-04-8
PEOPLE, a collection of short stories 1988 cloth
ISBN 0-88962-350-3

Co-author
MANY FACES, MANY SPACES - ARTISTS IN ONTARIO
PROFESSIONAL MEMBERSHIPS:
ATA, American Translators Association
ATIO, Association of Translators and Interpreters of Ontario
P.E.N., A World Association of Poets, Playwrights, Publishers, Editors, Essayists, Novelists, Translators and Journalists;
TWUC, The Writers' Union of Canada; Women's Press Club of Toronto;
CAA, Canadian Authors Association;
EWG, Etobicoke Writers' Group'
AE, Arts Etobicoke

Olga M. DEY-BERGMOSER is a highly principled woman. She is very proud of her German father who, during World War II, paid dearly for his resistance to the Hitler regime in his native land. As did many of his countrymen, he spent three years in concentration camps, suffering indignities and severe deprivation for the sake of his convictions.

Olga was born in Holland. She grew up in austere wartime Germany. Her secondary schooling was provided by Ursuline Sisters in a Convent setting.

Following the war, her father equipped her with paints and brushes, encouraging her budding interest in art and - in high school - he took her along to visit art galleries. Together, father and daughter would analyze fine paintings so that she could learn to recognize talent and ability as exhibited by the Masters. These early introductions to the world of fine art, honed her appreciation and judgement.

Olga is the pure embodiment of enthusiasm and encouragement. She becomes totally involved in whatever interests her, and then focuses her effort on enabling others to earn recognition. Her interest in art and the promotion of artists is very strong and genuine. She recognizes and appreciates true talent and is always ready to applaud it.

In this volume. "MORE FACE, MORE SPACES - ARTISTS IN CANADA," twenty-two artists representing various art disciplines are showcased. The artists are drawn from across the country and from different ethnocultural backgrounds. The standard of art expression highlighted here is of the finest quality. Some of the artists are already well known and highly acclaimed while others will strongly benefit from this focus on their undoubted talents.

Our heartfelt thanks to all those idealistic Canadian artists who have so generously donated their time and given us free access to their material.

It is indeed a privilege and a pleasure to be able to serve the arts community.

In gratitude
Betty
and
Olga

HANDY ATMADJA

Meet Handy ATMADJA, an outstanding landscape painter and excellent amateur photographer; a globetrotter who draws his inspiration from settings all around the world.

Indonesian Sunset medium: oil dimensions: 41 x 61 cm

HANDY ATMADJA

This lively, dynamic artist was born in Djakarta, Indonesia, and has made Canada his home since 1977. Prior to his arrival in Canada, he was the director and owner of a department store in Surabaya, the second largest city in Indonesia.

He became interested in art when he was fourteen years old and was surrounded by a circle of outstanding artists who were his friends. Encouraged by their fervent enthusiasm, he started out with water colours and worked in that medium for almost one year. He then joined an art club and switched to oil painting, doing landscapes exclusively.

When the Second World War broke out, he totally abandoned painting until the end of the war.

Beginning in 1948, he studied for quite some time under the guidance of a well-known painter, the late Ernest Dezentje, who specialized in landscapes and many of those paintings are on display in the palace of the Indonesian President.

This artist, who is extremely fond of travelling, takes a sketchbook along wherever his trips may take him, never missing a chance. Whereas he used to paint on location in earlier days, he now makes an initial pencil sketch in black and white serving as basis for the oil painting which he does as soon as he gets home to his studio. However, amazingly enough, although he is a talented amateur photographer, he does not like to paint from photos unless he hasn't time to stop or stay long enough to do sketches on the spot. During his tours or travels, he takes photographs of the objects for the basic outline for his paintings. By sketching, he captures the atmosphere and colour combination to his satisfaction.

To expand his experience, he has visited art galleries and museums in London, Paris, Rome, Amsterdam, Brussels, Madrid, Moscow, Istanbul, Athens, the Balkan countries, Scandinavia, Asia, Australia, Brazil, Argentina, Mexico, and the United States of America.

Atmadja, who is a true nature lover, feels equally attracted to gently rolling land, bubbling brooks, glistening lakes, sparkling waterfalls, sandy beaches, rugged mountains and unspoiled wilderness clad in awe-inspiring silence. He thrives on scenic variety and that is also the reason why he fell in love with Canada where he finds grandiose settings of striking contrasts.

Bali on their way to the temple (original oil painting on Masonite; size incl. frame: 44 x 54 cm)

HANDY ATMADJA

Autumn Glory medium: oil dimension: 30 x 40 cm

Besides, to Handy, Canada has the most beautiful clouds and skies anywhere on earth. He feels this might be so because there are so many lakes and it could be the reflection from the water that makes the clouds so beautiful. He likes to sit for hours on end, contemplating the clouds drifting by.

This artist, who also has a talent for portraits, definitely prefers landscapes and two seasons in particular, namely summer and autumn since winter is too bleak and colourless for him. In his autumn scenes we can feast our eyes on intensely bright orange and various shades of yellow blending into a glorious setting, enhanced by extremely well balanced composition. These are scenes of striking realism. Some are dominated by a certain mood of nostalgia as, for instance, in his Balinese paintings with their exotic brilliance of colours that leaves a lingering impression in the mind of the beholder.

Atmadja comments: "Art makes me happy and relaxed." When he is in a happy frame of mind, his work just flows and he has never yet produced a painting driven by frustration or completed during depression. Once he starts painting, he forgets the whole world around him - food would not even enter his mind - and the hours simply fly past. He paints, on average, three times a week.

In Canada, he studied commercial art at the Mohawk College in Brantford from which he graduated in June 1983. On April 13th, 1983, the Board of Governors of that college gave him an Award for his superb oil paintings displayed at a Contest held in Hamilton.

Although Handy is an extremely busy person being an accomplished ballroom dancer and having

HANDY ATMADJA

Peaceful Lake medium: oil dimension: 46 x 51 cm

held many roles as extra in movies and television shows, he is also an amateur photographer, fond of tailoring, an active sportsman and gourmet cook, who always finds time for art and is rather prolific, producing twenty to forty paintings a year.

Sept. 22 to Oct. 2nd, 1988
Civic Garden Centre (Link Gallery) Edwards Gardens, Don Mills

November 1986
NYAC Gallery (North York Arts Council), a volunteer organization

Oct 1, 1985 to Oct. 30, 1985
Exhibition at the Pleasant View Library

July 9, 1985 to August 3, 1985
Exhibition at the Thornhill Community Centre

April 22, 1985 to April 26, 1985
Exhibition at the Taylor Place Open House
(A club for senior citizens, in Don Mills)

March 12, 1985 to April 12, 1985
Exhibition in the Credit Union Building, Toronto

Moraine Lake - Banff National Park, Canada original oil painting on Masonite medium: oil dimensions: 30 x 40 cm (incl. frame: 44 x 54 cm)

DIONE BORG

Meet Dione BORG, versatile oil painter whose specialty is portraits but who also does amazing still-life paintings, landscapes, abstracts and moving Biblical scenes.

(Excerpt published in the 1988 Summer issue of THE SPIRES Cultural Community Focus)

Self-portrait of the artist oil on canvas 28 x 36 ins.

This versatile artist was born in Malta in December 1952.

From the age of ten, drawing and painting clearly crystallized as a natural inclination of Dione's. Unfortunately, however, the curriculum at his high school did not provide any type of art instruction, so while sitting in class, his mind would drift at times and he would draw portraits. Of course, he was caught eventually but to his utter amazement - instead of being taken to task and punished - he received great encouragement from his teachers who liked what they saw, being obviously quite pleased with their portraits!

Also, Dione soon learned how to swap his sketches and drawings for things he fancied - a minor aspect - yet of major significance since it kept him drawing and painting in an environment in which art was practically non-existent.

Once he completed his secondary education, he attended an art school where he was given plenty of stimulus and incentives. He enrolled in a five-year programme. The first-year course was dedicated exclusively to drawing from classical Greek statues. He did mainly pencil drawings in those days but, later on, specialized in oil paintings - the medium with which he feels most comfortable.

DIONE BORG

Canadian Native Chieftain oil on canvas 30 x 36 ins.

Portrait of the artist's late father oil on canvas 18 x 24 ins.

At this young age Dione was often commissioned to do illustrations for books and television stations as well as stage sets - diversifications that added other dimensions to his art. He also enjoyed acting and writing poetry, but very soon the urge to paint grew stronger than any of the other interests and it became his lifetime commitment.

In 1969 he participated in a local group show featuring several of his oil paintings - this being his first showing in Malta.

In 1974 he entered a painting competition and the work he submitted, an early self portrait, actually led to his first One-Man Art Exhibition in 1975. One of the judges on the Board was so impressed with his work that she arranged for an exhibition of Dione's oil paintings covering mainly portraits, landscapes, and still-lifes. His enthusiasm was given a real boost when a visiting Armenian Ambassador, putting together a collection of art to be donated to his country as a cultural exchange, acquired one of his paintings. At almost the same time, the National Museum of Art purchased one of his portraits which was subsequently taken on tour to Paris to represent Maltese art abroad. Besides, a still-life painting was bought by the National History Museum.

Soon thereafter this artist emigrated to Canada and had to set aside his art for some time while struggling to eke out an existence. Once settled, he delved into portraiture - particularly Canadian Indians and Inuit - portraits that were shown in local galleries and sold out completely. His autochthonic art is extremely moving since he portrays Canada's native people in a state of innocence and with tribal pride in their eyes - in subdued earthy colours of ochre, brown, and warm hues of orange.

However, as with so many other artists, Dione has a regular profession which - luckily - is somewhat related to his inclinations. He specializes in interior design - a field in which great emphasis is placed on colour, space and harmony. Dione does derive great visual satisfaction from his work. On the other hand, there is one major disadvantage to his situation; he is not free to paint whenever inspiration moves him and sometimes he is simply too tired and worn out to paint after a full day's work, no matter how highly motivated he might feel.

As to the commissioned portraits, they are not so much a slavishly photographic representation of a likeness but more of a spiritualized rendition conveying the sitter's soul. Of course, there is a definite realism but no straightforward visual clinging to copylike transference. The artist expresses features through the medium itself. One can hardly take one's eyes off his portraits of elderly persons, done in gentle pastel colours with the characteristic lines of age softened by small patches of white highlights that conjure up an aura of wisdom and a touch of mystery.

Besides, he adapts his technique to the mood projected by the sitter using, for instance, a carefree technique to reflect casualness. He cannot tell exactly how long it will take him to finish a portrait because it all depends on when he reaches the point where his work starts to flow effortlessly, almost automatically.

He never follows a formula and tries to stay away from any restricting measures, as the belaboured and rigid goes totally against his grain. With fluid application of the paint, Dione tries to achieve a certain degree of complexity hoping that in an over-

Transfiguration oil on canvas 26 x 40 ins.

DIONE BORG

Still-life oil on board 24 x 32 ins.

all blending, the end result - the harmonious combination of the element of painting and subject matter - will provide enough visual and intellectual stimuli to capture the imagination of the viewer. For although they convey the freedom of expression which is of vital importance to the artist, Dione's paintings are not meant to be pieces of 'art for art's sake', without any sense of responsibility towards his social environment. They are rather a means of communication, a personal statement or observation about objects, people or events that have presented him with the initial source of inspiration.

Lately he feels like contributing something of a more universal scope such as religiously-inspired art. This became clear to him while he was doing a highly significant painting on the topic of TRANSFIGURATION, seeing it as the more subtle, psychological aspect of Christ. He presented it, using economy of movement and showing the metamorphosis from human to divine, with great emphasis on the play of light, thereby making a clear demarcation between supernatural and earthbound. The very earthly figures in the foreground are clad in bold, bright colours and are caught in an expression of awe, panic and bewilderment. On the other hand, Christ is depicted in sparingly applied soft hues of blue and white in a rather stylized manner, drifting away on a cloud in a sea of gold - the traditional colour symbolizing untarnishable glory.

In future, Dione hopes to have more time and opportunity to dedicate himself wholeheartedly to painting.

JANE COULSON HARDY

Meet Jane COULSON HARDY, ingenious designer, painstakingly accurate craftsperson to whom her craft is a work of love - a cheerful lady always bubbling over with new ideas and concepts.

"WELCOME TO MY WORLD OF EGGS," Jane greets me smilingly, displaying an assortment of exquisite globes with the landmasses shown in gold against a subtle off-white background; eggs with music boxes inside, eggs in the Fabergé style, eggs highlighting the Nativity scene, others with toy soldiers, some featuring wedding invitations, some again serving as birth announcements or for anniversaries, etc., etc.

The egg shells range from the tiny finch egg to large size ostrich eggs. Every single egg is beautifully decorated, coloured to match the occasion depicted and fashioned in a way so particular to Jane. Every single egg is a true piece of art.

"I've always worked with my hands - ever since I can remember. I started out by making clothes for my dolls, then dressing all the animals around me, sewing, doing petit point, embroidery, needlepoint, rughooking and ceramics."

About fifteen years ago she picked up a magazine, quite by chance, that had eggs depicted in it and she was hooked, since eggs had always fascinated her, symbolizing the source of life and fertility. The giving of decorated eggs has been an important tradition in the Old World for many years, expressing the love and friendship that lie deep in the heart of the giver.

But how was one to acquire the art of eggery and where could one get the supplies?

At first, Jane learned on a trial and error basis - starting literally from scratch. But then she was lucky enough to locate a lady in Kitchener who showed her how to cut the eggs and how to do the hinging. Of course, Jane no longer uses scissors but the proper tools. Since the acquisition of the secrets of the craft was not that easy, Jane swore that once she mastered the craft, she would share her knowledge with others. She now enjoys teaching everyone who comes to her showing genuine interest.

Having lost her mother at the tender age of two, Jane - although vulnerable underneath - turned rather independent and self-assured, endowed with a strong sense of fairness and willingness to share. Fear of competition is something alien to her character. She reasons quite logically, that it is most unlikely that any two people would come up with exactly the same idea and create totally identical pieces of work, especially if that type of work is truly a product of inspiration. On the contrary, Jane is rather pleased to exchange the DO's and DON'Ts of her craft. She believes that the more variety, the more enriching for everyone, and she is rather generous in her praise of other people's work. This

JANE COULSON HARDY

Ostrich Egg approx. 16" lengthwise
WELCOME TO MY WORLD OF EGGS

photo by Diran Frankian

generosity of mind stems from the magnanimity of her heart, for - amazingly enough - her most exquisite eggs have been gifts to others and had absolutely no price tag attached to them.

Jane regularly participates in the prestigious ONE OF A KIND show, held at the Toronto CNE. Prior to that, she was a regular participant in the Annual Pottery, Ceramics and Crafts Show at Circa Antiques and Interiors on Davenport Road.

She has demonstrated her craft across Canada and the United States. However, these shows generally involve quite a lot of work - usually 12 hours a day - for four or five days at a stretch leaving her very little time to practise her craft.

How does Jane conceive her ideas? Sometimes she awakens in the middle of the night, has an idea and can hardly wait to begin working on it first thing in the morning.

Often, someone will come to her and ask for an egg for a special occasion such as an anniversary. She will think about it and toy with concepts such as growth, symbolized through the use of trees or branches bearing family pictures.

She always feels particularly inspired by weddings, invitations to special events, and birth announcements. Once the feeling is there, Jane knows exactly what to do. Many of the eggs for special occasions are coated in mother of pearl to add an especially festive touch and lustre.

Smilingly, Jane comments: "You would hardly believe it - but people just love to have their pets immortalized on eggs and they don't at all mind the cost involved."

In a way, Jane's eggs are an affordable, modern-day homage to Fabergé - a rather harmonious craft of precision work in which everything flows smoothly together.

Take the triptych-like Christmas decoration, for instance:

a richly ornate golden stand cradles an opulently decorated egg lined with crushed velvet and trimmed with gold lace on perfectly cut and hinged stained panels - stained rather than plainly coloured - in order to enhance the artistic effect.

Jane's eggs are not only aesthetically pleasing but also perfectly structured - everything has to be carefully cut to fit precisely together.

An egg is one of nature's simplest shapes.

JANE COULSON HARDY

photo by Diran Frankian

Egg With Geisha Motif regular goose egg approx. 9- 1/2"

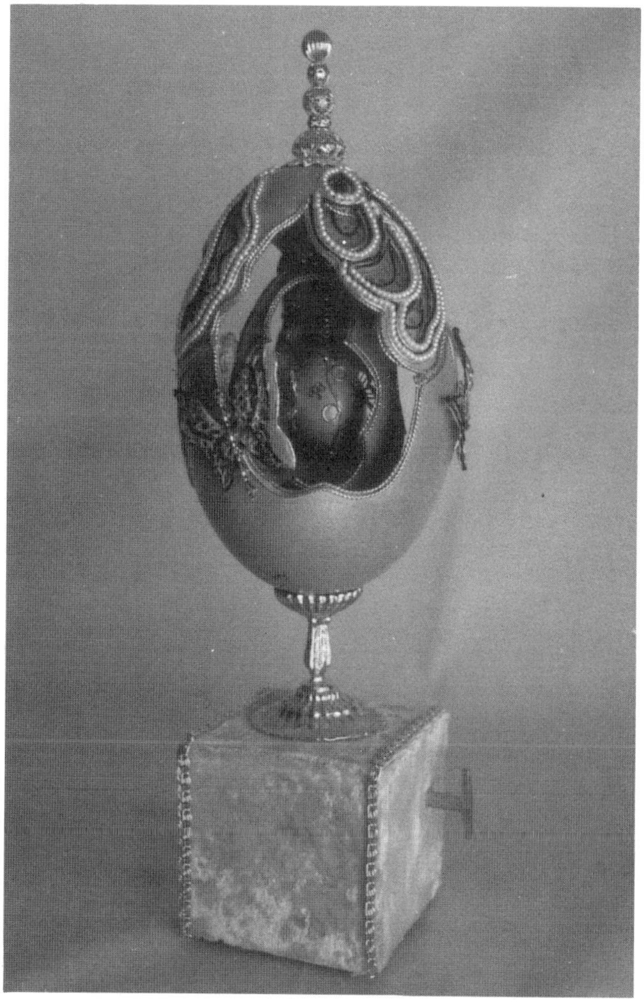

Blue (3 eggs in one) rhea, goose and quail eggs approx. 14"

JANE COULSON HARDY

Cabinet Egg that lights up osterich egg approx. 15-1/2"

photo by Diran Frankian

Christmas Egg total height: 12 cms double-yolk goose egg

photo by Diran Frankian

Jane's eggs look as if they were solid units, yet they open up to reveal delicate works of art hidden inside - for your eyes only.

Every one of her eggs is unique. Because they are hand-made, there are definitely no two eggs exactly alike. Every egg is a little gem for those who dare to look beyond what nature has given us - a little treasure you can close, or open up whenever you feel like looking at it so that it is indeed special to you every time you behold it. IT REALLY MAKES YOU WONDER WHAT CAME FIRST, THE EGG - OR THE INSPIRATION FOR THINGS OF BEAUTY - IN OTHER WORDS, THE IDEA FOR THE EGG.

What are Jane's dreams for the future? She has given craft demonstrations in churches and recreation halls where she was met with an overwhelmingly enthusiastic response on the part of the audience ranging from very young mothers to senior citizens. Having always enjoyed working with older children as well, Jane would really love to pass on her craft, sharing it fully with others. Lately, she has been teaching regularly on a private basis and is pleased with her students' positive results.

SOSY DIVIDIAN

Meet Sosy DAVIDIAN, with a special interest in minature art. Sosy was born in 1948 in the city of Jerusalem into a family with five artists and several craftsmen. Her father specialized in design and jewellery engraving in gold.

Cathedral medium: oil on canvas dimensions: 63 x 75 cm

She has been drawing since her childhood and, later on while studying the Arabic language, she would always draw in the book margins.

Sosy graduated from an Armenian high school in Jerusalem and was so fascinated with various styles of architecture and the restoration of antique works that she decided to attend the Beirut University where she enrolled in Fine Arts.

She soon realized that painting, graphics, and sculpting were her forte. Yet she felt, somehow, most at ease and confident in painting. However, her teacher suggested that she enter a piece of sculpture in an exhibition that was already featuring 14 of her paintings. She was actually quite shy about it and even felt rather reluctant about showing this particular sculpture, but what a surprise when she learned that it had not only won a prize, but had earned the top award!

Since then, she has had shows in Lebanon, Canada, and the United States.

Sosy usually painted in oil but since 1978, has been using India ink and gold leaf. Out of so many commissions, she especially enjoyed doing an Armenian war scene. This she painted from imagination and from having listened, over and over again, to the stories handed down by oral tradition. It is a grandiose work representing the Armenians struggling to form their own nation.

Work in ink and gold usually takes Sosy two weeks to complete.

Besides, Sossy's work is highly varied and

SOSY DIVIDIAN

Armenian Battle Scene medium: water colour, India ink & gold leaf dimensions: 35 x 26 cm

SOSY DIVIDIAN

intricate. There is, for instance, a village scene resembling tapestry-like depiction - yet actually modelled on a ceramic fresco. It is created using dynamic lines and rich colours - so many modulations of green - enhanced by a strong force of expression and energetic compositional flow.

Very early in her studies, Sosy became interested in old cathedrals that now lie in ruins in Turkish Armenia. Painstakingly, she studied photos of Armenian architecture going back 1500 years and more, and would then restructure these places of worship in her mind. She was fascinated with the massive arches and wide pillars and all the niches added on to the central structure, and she was intrigued by the effects of light and darkness.

For instance, when we look at her oil painting, CATHEDRAL, we feel transported to another world. Strong geometrical lines draw us right into the cathedral; solid parallel lines conjuring up massiveness of vaults. One is propelled into the corners and niches where the frosted blue and turquoise-coloured spaces, framed by silvery lines evoking stained glass windows, fill the viewer with tranquillity and serenity. This artwork features no ornamental details whatsoever. On the contrary, it is rather plain but with a strong compositional rhythm and upward striving thrust.

This versatile artist is also extremely interested in the sacred art of Islamic miniatures on which she spends endless hours of research. The illustrative decoration of absolute symmetry is of special appeal to her. In this discipline of art, all geometrical structures have to be as flawless as humanly possible, based on the principle that any communication with the Supreme Being has to take place in the most perfect manner imaginable. The use of lines and colours is highly restricted, the artist being limited to conventional or traditional styles.

The exclusively abstract designs are beautifully proportioned and perfectly balanced; designs

Village Scene medium: water colour and India ink dimensions: 42 x 23 cm

SOSY DIVIDIAN

so pure that no matter from which angle one looks at them they never lose their aesthetic compositional appeal.

Maybe this illustration with the central star-shaped panels, depicted within the larger rectangular format, best shows Sosy's fondness for this disciplined art form. The panels are surrounded by highly intricate decoration and an inscription in ornamental Eastern Kufic reads:

... This is the Koran handed down by God
in the form of a revered book
to be touched only by those who are pure of heart...

While at school, Sosy would sometimes sit there gazing out without any idea what she was going to embark on next. All of a sudden it would come to her. She would focus on a little atelier in an old building right opposite the school, surrounded by stone mansions. The window of the atelier had very old wooden frames; the glass was almost dirty, and it seemed to her that she was looking into a different world. Yet outside, she could see a garden that resulted, in this instance, in the oil painting entitled WINDOW.

To Sosy, the subject itself is not very important - but making something out of it - that's what interests her. Rather, she places her emphasis on extremely well balanced composition.

Sosy Davidian is an artist who combines the serenity of the past with the colourfulness of the present. Respecting the traditional East and the modern West. In doing so, she stands to be uniquely remarkable in her field.

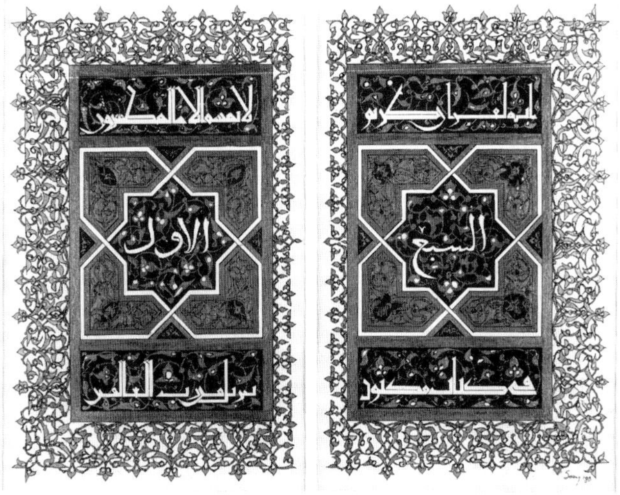

Pages from the Koran medium: water colour, India ink & gold leaf dimensions: 38 x 27 cm

MARIA GABANKOVA

Meet Maria GABANKOVA, a God-gifted portraitist, scenic painter and poet whose hauntingly beautiful realistic artwork deeply stirs the beholder.

This great artist, who is graced with genuine love and compassion for mankind and with touching humility, sees the expression of art as one of God's gifts with, however, the responsibility to further develop it inseparably tied to this talent.

May her own words as to how she feels about what the world expects of artists, serve as introduction to this warmth-exuding, sparkling, multifaceted personality.

How does the world want
the true egocentric artist
to be?
To reflect the world
within and without
to dig deep inside the dangerous
blood alleys
for those who don't dare...

He devours the reflections
of which
he is a captive
and is devoured
by his own consuming fire

and somehow arranges
the most elusive fragments
of reality
into
a silence
or a scream.

And these days
the true egocentric artist
should work darkly
for apocalypse is in vogue
and most likely we are already there -
to hear nothing
but our own cries.
With nothing behind Death,
the dark knight
with light footsteps
and sudden arrivals.

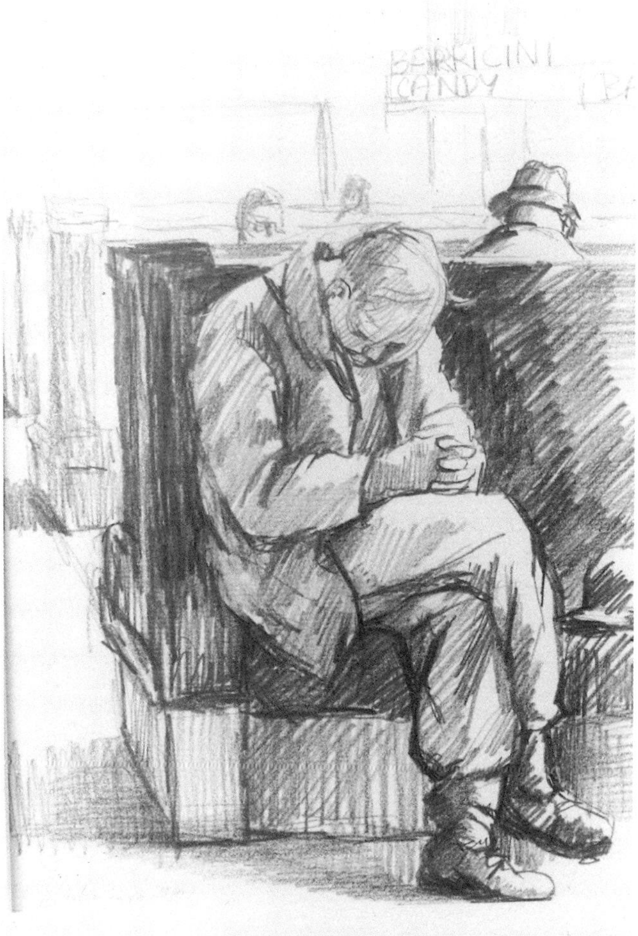

In Grand Central Station, (New York) medium: pencil dimensions: 9 x 12 ins.

MARIA GABANKOVA

Portrait of Corinne Boyer medium: oil dimensions: 24 x 32 ins.

Sometimes, the unusual does happen in life and a child is blessed with art, so-to-speak, in the cradle. Such was the case of Maria Gabankova who was born in 1951 in Czechoslovakia to Mr. and Mrs. J. Gabanek, outstanding portrait and landscape artists who graduated from the Prague Academy of Fine Arts.

Maria grew up surrounded by art, nurtured in art, appreciating art, and she has been drawing - along with her brother Jan - ever since her childhood, lovingly encouraged by their parents. "They have given me so much - something so very precious," she comments, displaying some works of tranquillity and serenity painted by her parents.

Maria, who has been living in Canada since 1968, initially studied art in her homeland where she was enrolled with the Ostrava Art School from 1966 to 1968. Then at the impressionable age of 17 - following the Soviet invasion in 1968 - she came with her parents to Vancouver.

In 1970 she graduated from the Kitsilano High School in Vancouver and then, following a year of studies at the University of British Columbia, Dept. of Fine Arts, she spent almost one year in the south of Spain.

She returned to Canada where she continued her studies at the School of Art and Design in Montreal, from where she returned once again to Vancouver to enrol at the Vancouver School of Art, studying, at the same time, figure and portrait painting with her parents. She would draw from models, supported by her parents' critique.

It didn't take Maria a long time to realize that the school was strictly abstract - too abstract for her taste - totally devoid of any figurative or conceptual art whatsoever.

In her spare time, she did innumerable sketches, drawings, etchings, lithographs and woodcuts, and was twice awarded the Helen Pitt Scholarship. She graduated, majoring in printmaking.

Old Fisherman medium: charcoal portrait by Joseph GABANEK, Maria's father, by whose refined figure painting and highly perfected portraiture she was greatly influenced

MARIA GABANKOVA

Gone were the days of nostalgic sepia sketches with open doors shedding light on domestic life, and touching depictions of mother and child in softly flowing, reassuring lines! She was now driven to open up a different world to the beholders of her sketches; a world of the underdog, the skidrow bum, catching a wino on the momentary upbeat with a glint in his eye while there are still a few drops left in the bottle in which to drown his grief and sorrows.

With moving compassion she drew, for instance, a woman - obviously at the crossroads of her life - her head buried in her marked hands. More and more realistic scenes followed.

No one who has ever seen Maria's painting of a group of elderly men hanging around in Grand Central Station in New York, can ever forget it. And those who know her poetry will automatically remember:

... my heart is a railway station
where people almost meet
and leave a steam sigh of all the distant cities
they touched
and their eyes have travelled across the super
sonic jet skies...

It is the human fate that fascinates her since it is so character-forming. It is as if she were rediscovering the saying that "At twenty you have the face that God gave you but at forty you have the face you deserve." She reads people's faces in the same way others read books - and she tries to freeze their expressions - but for a fleeting moment in time.

Being an immigrant herself, her painting, IMMIGRANTS, is perhaps one of her most penetrating pieces of work. It shows despair, resignation and a flicker of hope and promise in the eyes of the woman who is trying to come to terms, whereas the male stares into the distance being hurt, alienated and oh so lost.

In 1979, Maria moved to New York, joined the Arts Students League where she studied with G. Rahberger, F. Mason, R.B. Hale, and D. Leffel, and it was there that she copied the great Masters such as Rubens, Van Dyck and Murillo - just to mention a few - at the Metropolitan Museum of Art.

After her return to Vancouver she felt, all of a sudden, irresistibly drawn towards sculpting and took classes at the Fraser Valley College in Abbotsford, with Heinz Klassen.

Kafka's Prague, 1988 medium: oil dimensions: 28 x 22 ins. (presented to the Czechoslovak President Vaclav Havel during his 1990 visit to Canada)

Yet, in the course of time, a fascination with the human figure and face, in particular, had crystallized. Having done portraits off and on, Maria now knew beyond a doubt that portraiture was her specialty.

And how does Maria do those hauntingly moving portraits? First of all, she spends some time with the person so he or she can be totally at ease and uninhibited. Only once she has figured out the most natural and comfortable position for the sitter, does she embark on doing sketches - a process that may vary from two to five sittings depending on the size of the canvas and whether or not the sitter moves frequently. If all the conditions are right, she can work very fast and - as she admits - she is at her best when proceeding quickly.

"There is a lot of pressure and tension at first because I want to penetrate the mysteries hidden underneath the human face, the exterior veneer wanting to capture the true personality - going far beyond the purely visual elements of the painting itself. Consequently, I have to try and block out the feeling of the person and must ignore what they are expecting to see because we only know ourselves through the reverse image reflected from the mirror but not how another person perceives us."

MARIA GABANKOVA

Lost Lagoon medium: watercolour dimensions: 24 x 18 ins.

"'But isn't that a nerve-wracking challenge?"
"'To some extent - yes. But don't forget, on the other hand, anything I see in the person goes right through me and is revealed in the painting, showing in the face."
'Maria aims at the inner person - the obviously visual being interesting but not half as interesting as capturing a person's soul.
"'And hands are such a very important part of a person," she adds, "They tell you a lot about the person - in a subtle way."

"Such expressive hands!

"You know, I love the language of hands - did you ever notice how usually one hand is active, and the other, passive. In most people, one hand is usually doing something whereas the other one is more relaxed. I am simply spellbound by hands since they reveal the duality and tension found in every human being."

No wonder that Maria has had so many solo exhibitions and has participated in innumerable group shows in Canada and the USA, winning prizes with her work. She is featured in European as well as North American collections.

In 1987 she won a prize in an exhibition held at Casa Loma and from December 12th to December 31st, 1987, also had an exhibition at the Czechoslovakian Baptist Church in Toronto.

CHRISTA GRAF

Meet Christa GRAF, painter and creator of powerful sculptures, brightening our conflict-torn world with her aesthetically appealing artwork.

Madonna medium: cedar dimensions: 15 ins.

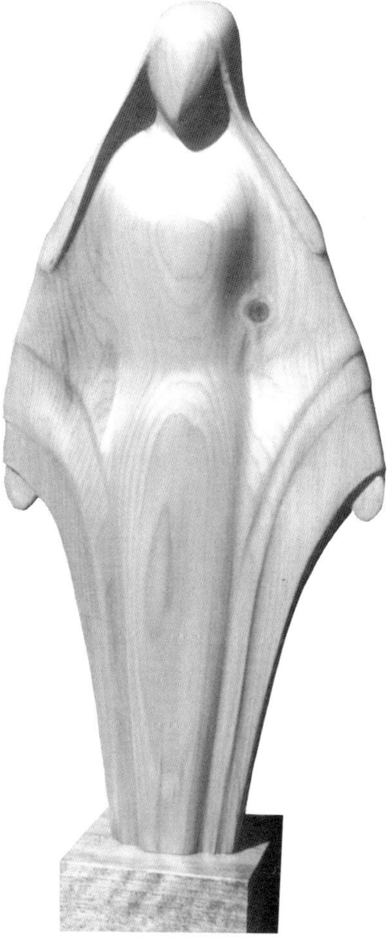

Christa was born in Germany on Christmas Day in 1934. Since her early childhood she has enjoyed art which was one of her favourite subjects throughout school. She did quite a few abstract paintings, sometimes based on her bizarre dreams. To her surprise, those pictures were always appreciated by older friends and family acquaintances. During her teens Christa was - apart from painting - also involved in acting. She would sometimes play the lead role in school or group plays in her hometown and there was no greater satisfaction for her than having the audience enjoy these plays.

The month of December seems to be truly crucial for Christa. In December 1956, she came with her parents for a visit to Canada. They were to settle with her older sister who was already living in Toronto. She had planned to stay for a few months before returning to Germany to be married. However, fate dealt her a terrible blow. First of all, her father took ill on his crossing to Canada. He had to be hospitalized on arrival at Quebec City where he died five days later. Secondly, a fatal accident took the young life of her fiancé in Germany. That changed her entire life. Christa abandoned herself to art in order to cope, somehow, with this terrible, devastating loss - gradually finding solace in the beauty of art.

Initially, she plunged herself mainly into drawing and painting but then decided in favour of a formal approach through rather structured studies. From 1958 to 1964 she studied drawing and oil paint-

CHRISTA GRAF

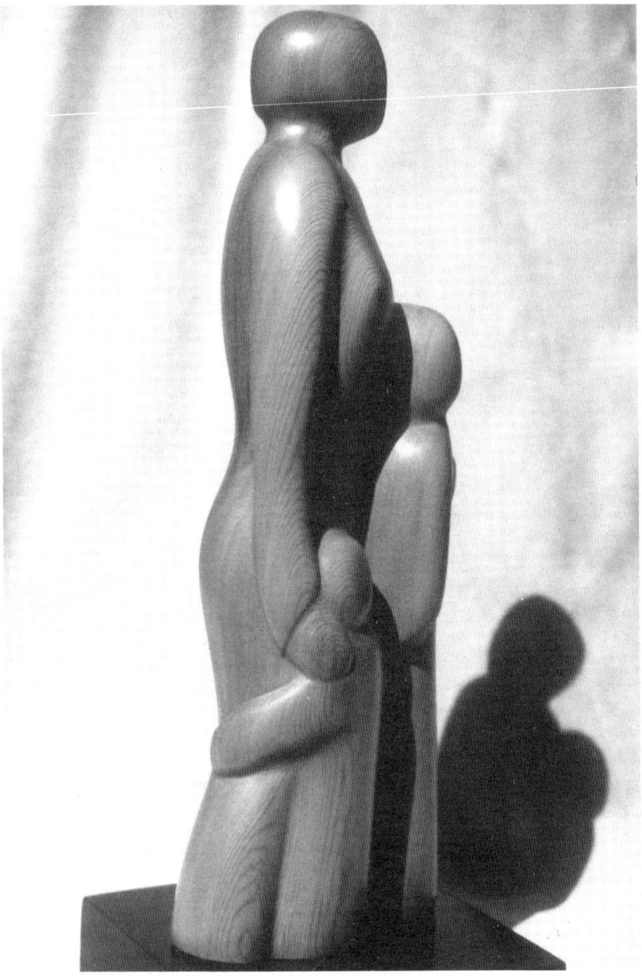

Single Parent *medium: cedar* *dimensions: 13 ins.*

ing (still life, figure drawing and portraits) at Northern Secondary school under Albert Jacques Franck and Don Fraser. Passing the sculpture class all the time and seeing other students modelling and casting, so intrigued Christa that she enrolled in sculpture as well - on different nights - studying from 1961 to 1964 at the same school under Frances Gage and Margaret Graeb.

From 1965 to 1967 she took up sculpture at Central Technical School under Augustin Filipovic.

Many summer vacations were spent at the Schneider School of Fine Arts. There, teachers such as Mary Schneider, Jack Pepper, Jack Pollock, Adrian Dingle, Aba Bayefsky, Guttorn Otto, Don Fraser, Carl Schaefer and John Gould helped form her artistic talent.

Since Christa derives such immense pleasure from art, she was eager to share this with others when she was asked to teach elementary oil painting during evening courses at Winston Churchill Collegiate in Scarborough from October 1968 to March 1971 - classes that proved to be mutually enjoyable and enriching to teacher and students alike.

During 1979 it became obvious to Christa that it was impossible to devote herself to all the areas of art that she had studied. She had limited time at her disposal, forcing her to restrict her endeavours. Following a careful deliberation, she opted in favour of sculpture as her main activity, with pencil or ink drawings as the odd diversion. She went back to Central Technical School, where she now studied wood carving under Lanny Shereck from October 1980 to March 1981 and - on a different night - bronze casting under Richard McNeil.

In the Fall of 1980, Christa made the big decision to live on her savings for a year and devote all

Family *medium: cedar* *dimensions: 16-1/2 ins.*

CHRISTA GRAF

Soapstone carving on pine dimensions: 8-1/2 ins. high

her time to wood-carving and sculpture. She moved to Lakefield where a friend had offered her a house, allowing her to get away from the distractions and hectic social life of the big city and to create undisturbed. This proved to be a very fulfilling time in Christa's life.

She did confirm to herself that wood carving was her special love. When not carving, she would be outdoors, sketching and drawing from nature. She also took part in two weekend seminars at the Buckhorn School of Fine Art under Christine Wilson, with special emphasis on pen and ink in colour.

Once back in the city, she studied woodcarving with Warren VanEvery at the Cedar Ridge Studio from September to May 1982, '83, and '84 and, at the Midland Avenue Collegiate, from October to May 1984, '85, and '86, learning the techniques for bas and high reliefs. In September 1983 she rediscovered her former teacher, Frances Gage, who has a studio on Birch Street in Toronto. Christa has been joining

CHRISTA GRAF

her Tuesday night carving group ever since.

Although she has been working since 1961 with clay sculpture, cement fondu and a few wood carvings, she works nowadays almost exclusively in wood and - with classical music in the back-

Despair medium: bronze on marble
dimensions: 5 1/2 ins. high

ground - she loses all sense of time and gets deeply involved in her work.

"It's so nice to work with wood," she comments. "It's such a warm and living material and certain woods smell aromatic when you are carving them."

Once the love of wood might die a little or when she feels she might want to change, Christa will venture into stone. However, at the moment she only works in wood, preferring fruitwoods such as apple and cherry wood but also walnut or maple. They are nice and hard - have a beautiful grain - and are pleasant to carve.

Wood quite often dictates what one should do with it if it is shaped in a certain way. However, it can also pose a challenge to your creative mind. If you have a straight tree trunk - you can allow your imagination a free hand and might come up with a head, a torso or an abstract form.

One thing Christa firmly believes in, is family unity and its sanctity, a belief that led to the creation of some of her most touching sculptures. Besides, she enjoys doing human figures - irrespective of whether they are stylized or realistic as long as you can somehow recognize the human form. However, when it comes to animals, Christa definitely likes them stylized rather than super realistic Slavish copying goes against Christa's grain.

Does Christa nurture any special dreams?

She would like to have a little house in the country and be able to do her sculpture on a full-time basis. Besides, she would like to create many pieces so that she could have a show every year. She hopes to create sculptures that are pleasing to the eye - nothing drab or ugly - as she feels there is already enough of that in our conflict-torn world. So why not create something pleasing?

Her work is very successful. Between December 1965 and December 1989 she had nine one-woman shows, most of which included paintings, drawings, and sculptures.

Apart from that, she has participated in about 15 group exhibitions such as the Toronto Mendelsohn Choir Art Sale, Grace Church on-the-Hill Art Sale, Beth Tikvah Sisterhood Art Sale, Colour and Form Society, Cliffcrest United Church Community Show, the Buckhorn Wildlife Art Festival, and the CNE Woodcarving Show. Christa was also represented at the Lakefield Art Shows (Lakefield Celebration of Fine Art) in July 1987 and in 1988. Besides, she had a one-woman SCULPTURE & DRAWINGS exhibition at the Cedar Ridge Creative Centre in Scarborough from October 23rd to 28th, 1989.

This artist has been represented by: Juliane Galleries of Fine Art, Toronto - 1969-1972; The McDowell Gallery, Toronto - 1981-1983; Whitman Gallery, Toronto - currently.

Her work can be found in private collections in Canada, Germany, Morocco, and the United States.

ELVA & EDGAR HASSELFELDT

He who works with his hands is a labourer,
He who works with his hands and his head is a craftsman,
He who works with his hands, his head, and his heart is an artist.
St. Francis of Assisi

Did you ever walk into a home where every single room abounds in art? Well, if not, then you simply must meet Edgar and Elva, a unique couple in whose hands everything turns into art.

You can feast your eyes on elegantly embroidered napkins at a table generously decked with culinary delights, on tapestry, on firescreens and bell-pulls of matching design by Elva, and ceramic plates out of North York clay and striking paintings by Edgar. On closer scrutiny, his artwork reveals the influence of the powerful Group of Seven, which is not surprising as Edgar actually studied under A.J. CASSON, the last living member of that group.

And then there are portraits. The one of his son is of such penetrating depth you can almost guess what the sitter was thinking at the moment the father froze his likeness in time.

Edgar also does sculptures and they are of such clean sweeping lines you just can't take your eyes off them. The TWO LOVES sculpture in marble and serpentine is especially impressive in its stunning simplicity. The face of an oriental woman, Fan Su, is shrouded in an atmosphere of mystery.

The bronze sculpture of Nefertiti does full credit to this Egyptian queen.

Edgar, who just couldn't live without art, went to work in the mines in order to finance his studies at the OCA (Ontario College of Art). He enrolled in a full-time general course in pottery, sculpture and painting for three years but then had to interrupt his studies during the war. While only in his late twenties, he was already a Warrant Officer in charge of a Naval Instrument Shop in Dartmouth, having 150 subordinates report to him. Right after the war Edgar re-enrolled with the OCA, taking night courses, but eventually went back into industry.

Yet, as if all this diversity weren't enough, Edgar also enjoys art photography, cabinetmaking and - last but not least - is a renowned gem cutter and jeweller. Actually, his prestige in this field is

photo by Diran Frankian

Meet Elva and C. Edgar HASSELFELDT, both extremely talented artists who create side by side - in total harmony.

With Edgar's portrait of their son Alan in the background medium: oil dimensions: 20 x 26 ins.

such that some of Toronto's best known jewellers come to him for advice, help and repairs if mishaps should occur at their end with cutting and setting.

As you walk along the hallways in this gracious home, you will notice lampstands created by this artistic couple and rugs featuring Islamic motifs of perfect symmetry - a true labour of love. Elva spent years of research studying all the background literature she could find on tapestry design.

She immortalized Norway, for instance, with its fjords and Lapp inhabitants in tapestry all worked in wools - sod roofs with seeds and springflowers bursting out of them; Greece - with a scene from Santorini, its snowwhite abodes and winding ascending cobblestone lanes and, above all, Colombia - with a special sense of humour. It was so hot in Cartagena that Elva had to go inside where she created a very amusing, most colourful, indigenous-looking piece of tapestry featuring the face of the devil symbolizing the hellish sun. She also made Bolivian masks. Yes, her tapestry is truly representative of so many parts of the world.

A propos masks, her Canadian masks - particularly the Haida masks originating from the west

photo by Diran Frankian

Untitled painting showing the influence of the Group of Seven medium: oil dimensions 23 x 31 ins.

Sculpture Two Loves medium: marble and serpentine dimensions: 20 ins. high

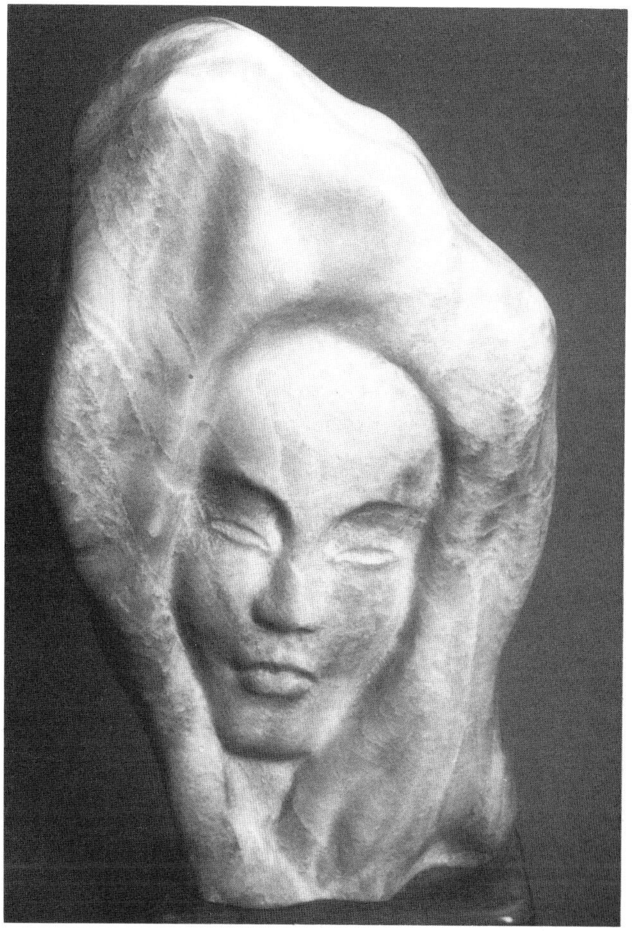

photos by Diran Frankian

Fan Su medium: marble dimensions: 14 ins. high

coast - are masterpieces 'sans egal,' and there is nothing dated about them. These masks are rather modernistic and every part is highly significant, as Elva patiently explains. They were created to bring the rain, to stop the rain, to produce fertility, etc. Elva, who carefully studied the Haida masks, adds couleur locale by using shells from the region and interweaving hair (horse hair). You can feel those masks - they are captivating and exude a power all their own.

She has also done quite a few animal tapestries with a see-through effect. This is in keeping with the belief that the spirit sees through everything and that there is absolutely nothing you can ever hide.

Walking along, Elva kindly points out the natural progression of colours in her Jacobean tapestries. That particular kind of art focuses on "cool colours" but the artist must always depict some life such as owls, butterflies, etc. However, the proportions are totally unimportant in this special artform. Elva's talent is such that she can change from details to broad style and vice-versa, without any problem.

Suddenly we come to a room featuring Edgar's modern paintings. I am struck by artwork of touching symbolism highlighting the topic of peace and conflict. Out of closely entwined, vibrating circles - turmoil and chaos - rises the head of a woman, madonna-like, dispensing peace.

Besides, there are several mood scene photographs. Edgar ventured into art photography many

ELVA HASSELFELDT

years ago - with a box camera - while still a teenager, and he won several awards - mostly for his landscapes.

And then - a collection they started 25 years ago - of fossilized stones. It includes 10-million year old shark teeth (they had them dated in Maryland) and even a fossilized Dinosaur bone - out of a dry desertlike climate - well preserved, petrified, almost beyond time's merciless clutches of destruction.

While showing this collection, they were both bubbling over with enthusiasm, reminiscing the innumerable field trips that they had taken together and the many years they'd spent on research. They usually go canoeing in the summer and look for and

Prayer Rug medium: wool dimensions: 28 x 48 ins.

photos by Diran Frankian

Haida Mask Tapestry medium: wool and wooden beads dimensions: 48 x 28 ins.

find very beautiful and unusual pieces of wood and stone. They avidly collect rocks on location and Edgar, who is an expert in sawing and slicing rocks, cuts and polishes them, creating almost any shape he wants - making the most amazing jewellery.

"Nature abounds in art," he modestly comments. "The potential is almost too vast for the human mind to visualize."

One has to admit, it takes a very special and trained eye to see that a simple rock an average person would ignore - would not even bother to look at - may enclose a precious gem.

Edgar then shows me the studio where he teaches gem cutting, faceting and setting. I am fascinated with a special saw with diamonds on the edges that slices through any kind of rock. Fortunately, this artist learned tool and die-making and specialized as an industrial designer, a trade that

EDGAR HASSELFELDT

photos by Diran Frankian

Wood Stump Tapestry medium: natural wooden stump and mushroom in wool
dimensions: wood 14 x 10 ins. mushrooms 6 ins.

proved to be an enormous asset for jewellery-making. It also allows him to make many machines to suit his specific needs. He can thus circumvent any problem because of his solid background knowledge and his mastering of metal techniques.

Both of them believe in extreme self-discipline and conscientious taste development. There are no shortcuts. There is no such thing as instant success. Neither is great artwork a question of luck, but rather the result of persistent struggling. On the other hand, both are also convinced that they can create whatever they wish to make, emphasizing the harmony of perception and creativity.

What does Elva contribute to Edgar's unique jewellery? - She proudly wears it.

When they first came to know each other, Edgar would take Elva to art galleries and, usually, those visits were followed by extensive discussions. Somehow though, Elva would mentally frame everything she saw as if it were meant for her livingroom until Edgar - intrigued by her rejection of certain artwork - discovered this 'frame of mind' and then - with his loving guidance - led Elva to total freedom of art within the widest scope possible.

Just as Edgar has his workshop, Elva has her own studio where she draws her designs on background material. Next, she cuts strips of white 100% pure wool - 3" x 12" - which she then dyes in a variation of eight colours. After the dying process, she puts them in a little cutter and makes them into strips of about 1/8" wide. She is extremely organized, keeping all the various shades and nuances of colours neatly sorted. She expands her tapestry by using different textures and colours in yarns which project the desired special effect.

Her rustic tree stump tapestry with mushrooms and that of fruit with flowers are particularly appealing, and she won the Chatelaine Magazine Award for a group of four, with mushrooms as the motif.

She did, for instance, a tapestry of teasels (originally brought over from Europe to tease wool as with a brush or comb) and it is so realistic that you are tempted to reach out and touch it.

Elva's tapestry ranges from the traditional to the very modern and is, indeed, an absolutely unique expression of creative hooking.

Elva and Edgar have both been teaching for quite some time. Edgar taught gem cutting at the

ELVA & EDGAR HASSELFELDT

photos by Diran Frankian

Yellow gold ring with blue topaz and diamonds

medium: natural wooden stump and owl in wool
dimensions: 22 ins. wood stump 12 ins. owl

George Brown College for 5 years and ceramics at various schools for eight years. Elva taught tapestry for about twenty years but is retired now. Edgar is still accepting private students who are seriously willing to learn.

Edgar and Elva are both extremely observant and always tell aspiring artists to observe and explore because they feel that you have to be able to relate before you can create.

Both of them have participated in many exhibitions and Elva was actually the first woman ever to have a one-woman demonstration at Hart House. Besides, Elva and Edgar were both representing Ontario craftsmen at the Montreal Olympics in 1976 where Elva had many tapestries on display at the Place Bonaventure ARTISANAGE Exhibit. At the same place, Edgar showed the techniques of gem cutting.

Furthermore, in the Make Show at the Ontario Science Centre, Elva had a bell-pull featured that won an award.

Some of Edgar's jewellery is part of the display at the Jean A. Chalmers permanent collection. It went on tour for two years before ending up in Ottawa in her private collection.

At the Entr'acte Show at the O'Keefe Centre under the motif of THEATRE, both of them jointly participated, Edgar with a piece of jewellery - a necklace entitled LEADING LADY - and Elva, with a bell-pull entitled YOU RANG, MADAM?

Seeing two such enormously talented artists work side-by-side without any resentment, but rather bound together by enthusiasm and loving support - makes one feel that this world is still a wonderful place in which to live. Together, they are truly a guiding light to others.

SUZANNE KRALKA

Meet Suzanne KRALKA, née RANGER, this vigorously vibrant, boldly innovative painter, sculptor, and mask maker.

With worldwide travel experience - a true federalist imbued with a glowing love for Canada, a Quebecoise who served as volunteer at the TORONTOLYMPIAD for the Handicapped in 1976, an entertainer par excellence who just loves to see people happy and make them laugh.

Being the youngest of eight children of a Lachine-based family with definitely no extra money floating around to be spent on any training in art, Suzanne, who always enjoyed drawing and painting, had to patiently wait for a long time until she was able to take her first art class.

Yet nothing ever managed to smother her dream nor could anything put a damper on her hope and ebullient enthusiasm in the meantime, for no matter what, Suzanne is always bubbling over with joie de vivre. Besides, she enjoyed her husband Peter's full support at all times.

She married, created a cozy home and became the mother of two lovely daughters, Louise and Johanne. Louise was a dancer with La Compagnie des Ballets-Jazz de Montreal whereas the youngest opted for social work, childcare for children in difficulty being her life's mission.

Suzanne, with the passion for art pulsating in her veins, was only temporarily subdued by life's circumstances because defeat is something she simply doesn't know. Her circle of friends always comprised a fairly large number of artists. Besides, she would eagerly devour books on art and gather impressions on her trips around the world (without

Bust of Daughter Johanne when she was 17 years old

SUZANNE KRALKA

Sculpture - Modèle barbu (bearded model)

any photographic recording) which she would carefully store in her memory bank of later application and further elaboration.

Only when her children were of school age, did Suzanne - for the first time - enrol in a night class in Lachine held by a professor from the Musee des Beaux Arts. Being a joiner and a doer, she enjoys taking courses and attending workshops which allow her to exchange ideas with classmates. Wherever she is, she contributes to bringing about a stimulating atmosphere. She is totally devoid of aggressive competition. Instead, she is a great advocate of healthy collective growth. Although she works mainly on her own, Suzanne needs the motivation of a group from time-to-time as she likes to be among inspired artists where the air vibrates with creativity.

This very diversified artist dares her imagination to run wild <<developper l'imagination à la limite>> as she calls it. She started out with still-life and - subsequently - engaged in monoprints with special emphasis on texture, composition, and thinness of paint. She enjoys sculpting and every piece Suzanne creates is a joy to behold.

Suzanne uses all kinds of media such as pastel, oil, acrylics, and gouache and, last but not least, even housepaint. She has, furthermore, done innumerable collages. However, she has a special innate talent and predilection for sculpture - the power of expression reflecting her gift of penetration. Her sculptures are people you and I know; people with such clear features we can easily relate to them. They are so plastically appealing that they transcend because this talented artist knows how to breathe life into them. Of course, she has immortalized members of her family in clay and the bust of her youngest daughter, Johanne, was on display for quite some time.

Then, one day, one of her daughters presented her with a book about the Kau tribe in the Sudan. She was so fascinated by the way the men of the tribe so artistically masked their faces with paint that she reproduced their faces in clay but masked them in her own style, yet under their influence.

People became very interested in her work and - from May 13th to June 20th, 1984 - she had her first exhibition on MASKS at the Sarto Desnoyers Cultural Centre in Dorval (Service Loisirs et Culture). The exhibit was highly successful.

SUZANNE KRALKA

Masks

Intrigue medium: collage on canvas combined with acrylic and felt pen dimensions: 13-1/2 x 16-1/2 ins. featuring two women transcending normal existence

Suzanne had the brilliant idea of hiring a mime to fittingly open the exhibition. Individuality and originality - thy name is Suzanne!

And there is no limit to her experimental work. She gets, so-to-speak, swept off her feet - artist and artwork blending into one - resulting in something challengingly unique; something so intense with energy that she addresses us directly through her work, stating:

<<J'aime ce que je fais,
je le vie,
je suis heureuse.>>

Then in the Fall of 1985 when the Picasso exhibition was held in Montreal, Suzanne fell totally under his spell. She adores Picasso for his enormous energy and the feeling of motion he conjures in the beholder. Besides, she admires his uniqueness and whimsical playfulness. We suddenly notice a progressive tendency towards abstraction in Suzanne's

SUZANNE KRALKA

Under the Spell of Picasso

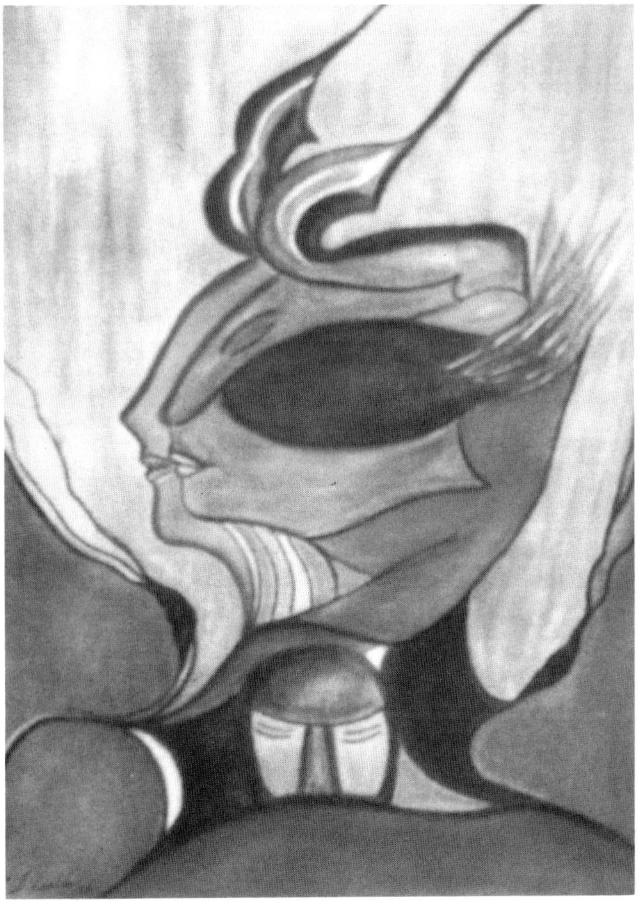

work. It, therefore, comes as no surprise that her work, entitled UNDER THE SPELL OF PICASSO, shows an amazing intensity of colour, a total disregard for realistic dimensions. Even the painting spills beyond its frame. Instead, she now conveys reality through illusion. Yet faces - for instance - that may seem almost naive or slightly absurd on the surface, feature, at the same time, penetrating eyes with much to reveal.

For the past two years she has been studying with the artist, Marion REVENKO, who initiated her to the wonders of contemporary art; an instructor who insists on individualistic creativity freeing her students from any restricting conventional approach. She opens up vistas of a different range of potential to them. However, heed the saying: <<L'homme se détruit à la recherche de l'absolu>>. "Don't head for perfection or the work may die on you."

"It's no longer a question of doing what you see, but doing what you feel. Emotions are involved. Today, a camera can capture beauty in a second. But to me, as an artist, to copy beauty is no challenge. It has already been done. It's already there. My camera took it."

This great idealist, full of love and compassion - with a long record of volunteer work involving, in particular, less fortunate children - creates timeless work that touches everyone.

From May 6th to May 27th, 1987, Suzanne had a one-woman show at the Dorval Cultural Centre featuring paintings, monoprints and sculptures, and guestbook comments such as .."IF MY WORLD HAD AS MUCH COLOUR AS YOUR ART, I WOULD SEE A RAINBOW"... and <<"JE VEUX FAIRE PARTIE DE TON AURORE">>... speak for themselves.

What is Suzanne doing right now? She is presently taking a course in PAINTING FROM THE SUBCONSCIOUS, exploring subconscious imagery in the process of individuation with emphasis on visual and tactile stimulation orientation.

What are her dreams? To found an artists' co-op studio.

Her concluding comments: "There is something to be said about great art - it passes from one generation to another and visually touches everyone."

VLADYANA KRYKORKA

Meet Vladyana KRYKORKA, a distinguished magazine designer and illustrator of cheerful, bright-coloured children's books that gladden your heart and make you anxious to read the story so intriguingly highlighted by Vladyana's artwork.

1988 Calendar medium: water colour and pencil dimensions: 7 x 7-1/2 ins.

This energetic and enthusiastic, yet simultaneously most humble artist, is truly an inspiration in herself and simply loves drawing people of any age and background. To her, physical age is of no major consequence as long as people are healthy and of good spirits. No wonder the parents and other older family members in the children's books she so aptly illustrates, have such a wide appeal.

Vladyana always wanted to draw. Luckily, her parents recognized, appreciated, and encouraged her talent at an early stage. They wholeheartedly believed in her and were genuinely supportive, sending her every Sunday afternoon to Professor Landa. Under his guidance, she drew flowers, painted landscapes and - later on - learned portraiture. She was merely eight at the time.

As soon as she reached the age of 14, she enrolled with a high school with special emphasis on art. That particular school had a four-year programme and is one of Prague's best art schools focusing on illustration and advertising.

Upon completion of her studies, Vladyana then worked for one year for a small advertising agency, doing posters. However, she still wanted to continue studying art or some closely related field. She was extremely interested in three-dimensional projects and, therefore, opted for architecure. When only 19 years of age, she already illustrated her first children's book entitled KOUZELNY DESTNIK, the Magic Umbrella. She now dedicated herself to

VLADYANA KRYKORKA

Book illustration for A Promise is a Promise medium: water colour and pencil

studying architecture. She had completed 3-1/2 years of the 6-year programme when the political situation in her homeland came to a head. For quite some time, Vladyana had been working each year on the farm of some relatives in Austria in order to perfect her knowledge of the German language. In 1968 she went for another visit and took a trip from there - together with her fiancé - to Italy. Her eyes still sparkle when she recaptures memories of Florence and Venice. Their trip couldn't have been planned more opportunely since it was there - while being out of the country - that they learned about Soviet tanks rolling into Czechoslovakia.

Without a moment's hesitation they approached the Canadian Embassy and were told they could fly straight to Canada. So, on September 20th, they flew to Canada and have been blissfully happy in their new homeland ever since. Vladyana calls their immigration to Canada the best decision they ever made.

When they first arrived, Vladyana did not speak one single word of English but she immediately took an intensive evening course of 6-month duration from 4 to 10 pm each day and, while still

VLADYANA KRYKORKA

studying English, applied to the OCA (Ontario College of Art) in the Fall of 1969. She was accepted right away on account of her previous training and studies.

There she enrolled in a Communication and Design course which she tremendously enjoyed. And while still in her third year, she started working for Holt, Rinehart and Winston during the summer of 1971 and - during the last year of her studies - worked for them on a part-time basis, illustrating textbooks.

Following her graduation from the OCA in 1972, she worked for one year on a full-time basis. At that time, the art director Bob Frank left and formed his own company. He asked Vladyana to join him. She worked for him for one year till the summer of 1973 when her daughter, Suzanna, was born. Since that time, she has been freelancing - and very successfully so - as graphic designer and illustrator of text and children's books. Once her children - a son and a daughter - are grown up and she will have more spare time, Vladyana intends to indulge more in fine art, painting flowers and landscapes.

So far, she has illustrated six children's books in Canada, namely: DOODLE THE POODLE (Holt, Rinehart & Winston of Canada, Limited); THE BIG YELLOW FROG, story by David Carefoot, (Three Tree Press); PLANTING SEEDS, story by Patricia QUINLAN (Annick Press Ltd.); A PROMISE IS A PROMISE, story by Robert MUNSCH & Michael KUSUGAK, (Annick Press Ltd.) ; WHUMP, story by Gail CHISLETT, (Annick Press Ltd.); BASEBALL BATS FOR CHRISTMAS, story by Michael

Book illustrations for, A Promise Is A Promise medium: water colour and pencil

VLADYANA KRYKORKA

Magazine cover illustration medium: tempera dimensions 7 x 7 ins.

ARVAARLUK KUSUGAK, (Annick Press Ltd.).

Vladyana is an enthusiastic illustrator who likes bright colours and plenty of movement to captivate the children's attention. It is, at all times, her foremost concern to put energy and sunshine into any project entrusted to her, bringing out the positive aspects. "Even a difficult story can be illustrated in an enticing way."

On the other hand, her swift artwork is also a matter of experience since again and again, she is commissioned to illustrate books that have to be out by a certain date - often, with very short notice indeed.

Another angle to which Vladyana attaches great importance is diversity because the taste of children is not yet that refined and discerning as that of adults who go more for detail. Many books, nowadays, offer quite an array of artists - sometimes up to fifty illustrators for one single book - to speed up the illustrating process and give various people an opportunity to make a living. After all, there are so many artists and only so much artwork around!

So far, Vladyana has illustrated 30 educational books; the covers of a mathematics book series; books from kindergarten to grade 6, mainly for Holt, Rinehart and Winston, Nelson Canada, Houghton Mifflin Canada Ltd., Oxford Press Publ. House, McGraw-Hill Ryerson, and Ginn & Co., including small books for independent studies and the colourful, oversized books - BIG BOOKS - classroom demonstration books to be shared by the primary teachers with their students.

Vladyana is also the designer of a trade magazine called BENEFITS, by Maclean Hunter Limited, coming out ten times a year. She has been doing it on a freelance basis for 9 years now. Meanwhile her work has been crowned with several awards and in 1983 - she won the Canadian Business Press Award for BEST COMPLETE ISSUE, the Kenneth R. Wilson Memorial, and - in 1987 - she won the Best Cover Award for the same magazine.

In addition, she also illustrates the cover for a food-service magazine, something she really enjoys since food is so pleasant to paint. It leaves so much scope for imaginative creativity as to compositional fluidity and appealing colour schemes.

However, she finds children's book illustration most rewarding. She honestly admits what an incredibly fantastic feeling it is to see your book on the shelf. Her husband couldn't quite comprehend this at first but decided, nevertheless, to come along when a book came out to share that special moment with her. They sat down for a long while, leafing through the book - page by page - and the feeling really got to him.

Luckily, Vladyana has travelled quite extensively and gathered many impressions on those trips, some of which we find reflected in her work. Ever since she illustrated A PROMISE IS A PROMISE, she has had one cherished desire to take a trip north to study the Inuit. This dream suddenly materialized in November 1989 when she flew to Rankin Inlet to study the Inuit way of life.

Meanwhile she participated in the show "FIVE OF THE BEST CHILDREN'S ARTISTS", March 3 - 31, 1989, at the Del Bello Gallery in Toronto, and her work was featured in an exhibition to assist the dawn of FREEDOM & DEMOCRACY IN CZECHOSLOVAKIA, held on April 1st, 1990, in Toronto.

ELLINIDHA LEPSENYI

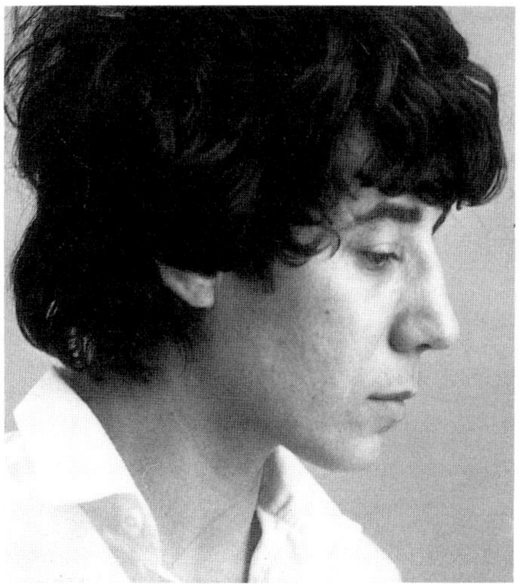

Meet Ellinidha LEPSENYI unique oil painter, [interview, with Ildiko VAS at the O.W.H. (Ontario Welcome House) kindly functioning as interpreter.]

Ellinidha was born on October 5th in Alap, Hungary. Having lost her father at a very early age, she ended up in an orphanage where she was left on her own a good deal of the time.

From the age of three she was drawn to art and kept a sketchbook that is still in her possession.

Being deprived of parents, she always wanted to get the attention of adults and desperately tried to win their affection. That's how she was driven to paint in the first place. She painted for adults to gain a way into their hearts.

Besides, she never grew tired of listening to them talking about sad things - problems of existence, marriage breakdown, etc. Then, too, she would paint hoping to alleviate the pain in their hearts by her pictures. It gave Ellinidha a very good feeling knowing that she could sense and understand their sadness and, through her paintings, manage to make them smile, even if only temporarily.

She never had a yearning for perfection though. When she painted a dog, for instance - and as a child she only painted animals - it was not the exact depiction or faithful reproduction per se that fascinated her. It was the idea that it was a dog you had cared for; a dog that was your friend or a dog you lost.

Once she attained the age of fourteen, she started to paint people exclusively and even today still keeps on painting people only.

Silence Within Herself/Silence Within the Milieu

medium: oil on wood dimensions: 67 x 67 ins. - the bleak background and oversized outstretched hand symbolizing alienation

ELLINIDHA I EPSENYI

Love medium: oil on canvas
dimensions: 80 x 60 ins.

Love in icey blue since it's not only frightening but can be downright terrifying, the most constructive and most destructive force (power) all at once.

ELLINIDHA LEPSENYI

While at the orphanage, she attended the internally operated elementary school but once she reached fifteen, she left the orphanage, found herself a job during the day and for four years attended high school at night, being particularly interested in literature. She graduated in 1972.

She now worked for a few months and then took off half a year to paint. She paints exclusively in oil. "Why only in oil?" one might ask. The artist had always admired Byzantine art and Greek murals in particular but she knew that her monetary situation was a serious drawback. Therefore, she studied the old Masters who painted mainly in oil. She really wanted to do something in art that had a long tradition.

When she was 21 years old, she was looking for a job and for the right person to help her, admitting in total honesty: "It's always a person you need - in any situation."

Luckily, she met a movie director who really liked her art-work and fully grasping her artistic penetration, gave her the job of film editor (1972-1986). With art coming naturally to her, what excitement to put a film together and get paid for the fun! She also functioned as assistant and would provide art objects as background for documentaries - her art really coming in handy in these instances.

Out of sheer curiosity, this artist learned the profession of film cutting and became a cutter in order to be able to keep on painting. In 1980, she applied for an entrance examination to the editing department at the College of Dramatic Art and Cinema and was accepted. She received her diploma in 1984. After that, she was in the employ of Hungarian Television.

On April 10th, 1981, Ellinidha had her first independent exhibition, and the second, on November 6th, 1985. So far, nineteen out of her 320 paintings exhibited, have been sold.

In 1986, she left for the Netherlands where she enjoyed her life to the fullest, experiencing a tremendous widening of her artistic horizon in a setting of total freedom, being exposed to all segments of society. During that time she did mainly portraits and puppets - well, yes, puppets - to teach people how to play, allowing them to be children once again. She is convinced that not only children should be taught to play. After all, there is a child hidden in every adult and people of all ages always need emotional involvement.

She also feels that children should not grow up being glued to a television screen but should be told moving stories that stir reaction - no matter at what age - no matter in which part of the world.

"There is something extremely moving about her people. They look helpless, hesitant, idle, just standing there - numb and bewildered - without companions but one senses they do have DREAMS."

It's a grandfather who already lived his life and all the people have a grandfather like him who tell stories be it about the first world war about amorous conquest of his youth about a life style that existed long ago, etc.

Grandfather Telling Stories 1968 medium: oil on wood dimensions: 50 x 40 ins. (The artist was only 15 years old when she did this painting.)

ELLINIDHA LEPSENYI

During her time in Holland she had an exhibition in the Permanent Exhibition premises of the Dutch Government in Den Haag.

In August 1987, Ellinidha came to Canada where - when she returns home from her English language classes in the mornings and afternoons - she eagerly paints. However, her funds are dwindling fast, a fact that makes her move a lot from one place to another - providing her with a constant change of scenery. Unfortunately, the fact that she has not yet mastered the English language causes special hardship in her case.

Yet despite penury, she consoles herself by thinking that it's a luxury to paint in this exciting part of the world. She knows she will never give up and will develop her art to the fullest in this beautiful, challenging new environment.

Existence medium: oil on wood
dimensions: 80 x 60 ins.

Existence in itself tragedy, awareness and hoping - a concept, not a definite depiction. Anyone can relate to it, since it's not the painting itself, but the feeling behind it, that matters.

Voluptuous figures oozing sexuality more dolls than real people no real depth of emotion no real feeling of sacrifice but to grasp, seduce, discard dream women but - amazingly
- without hands and arms
- to hold and embrace
- to cuddle and fondle
- to console and reassure
- to bless

Cicababak - "cat women" medium: oil on wood dimensions 40 x 60 ins.

MORE FACES
MORE SPACES

HANDY ATMADJA

DIONE BORG

JANE COULSON HARDY

SOSY DAVIDIAN

MARIA GABANKOVA

CHRISTA GRAF

EDGAR HASSELFELDT

ELVA HASSELFELDT

SUZANNE KRALKA

VLADYANA KRYKORKA

ELLINIDHA LEPSENYI

JOSE LOBO-FERNANDES

DEBORAH LOUGHEED

JIRINA MARTON

LOU POLLOCK

PASSIONARIA SECKA

ARNO SOLTESZ

MARGARET SPATARU

HARRY TANNER

ALEX TAVARES

INGA VON BOETTICHER

PETER ZOUDIS

JOSE LOBO-FERNANDES

Meet José LOBO-FERNANDES, a powerfully dynamic sculptor who never plans, but is always driven to create on the spur of the moment.

Family, 1990 (one of a group of several) medium: bronze dimensions: 97 cms

photo credit: Rev. C.L. Thompson

Born in 1921 in Mozambique, José LOBO-FERNANDES has been drawing and painting ever since he can remember.

Upon completion of his high schooling in Mozambique, he went to South Africa for two years in order to learn English since, in those days, it was much easier for English-speaking persons to find employment.

When he returned home, José found a job with the railways and that was when he first heard about the newly founded art school. He was immediately accepted. Although he was mainly interested in a programme in sculpture, unfortunately there was no such course available. The school offered, instead, a five-year programme in design and painting-oriented studies.

After some time he joined an art club where he met a great sculptor who taught him about anatomy, modelling and working with every kind of material (clay, plaster, wood, plastic, resins and fiberglass, cement, bronze, aluminum, etc.). Until then he had been painting mainly in pastels and oils.

JOSE LOBO-FERNANDES

He now totally abandoned painting in order to dedicate himself exclusively to sculpting.

José does not work in a given material but always adjusts the material to suit his concept. All artists see the same reality in a different way, having a differing intuition and vision, feeling and interpreting it subjectively. Besides, this artist creates on the spur of the moment and does not plan his artwork. He may do a sketch only to retain the idea and, therefore, never leaves his home without a sketchpad.

When showing me some of his sculptures, he told me that one day he was all excited because he had come across an old rugged, weatherbeaten fisherman with a most remarkable profile, clad in rags and tatters. His features were so clearly defined that he wanted him to pose as a model. He approached the man and, to his delight, the fisherman agreed. José set a date and happily paid him some advance. To his surprise - a few days later - this man came back to see him, cleanly shaven and in brand new clothes - scarcely bearing any resemblance to the character who had impressed José so deeply earlier. Needless to say, the artist's whole idea was spoiled. Bitterly disappointed but amused by the irony of life, José sent the man away.

Sometimes José did sketches in plaster, did the wiring for the shapes and worked directly in cement or fiberglass. Lately, he has been preferring fiberglass as his medium because of its light weight and the fact that it is, nevertheless, stronger than other materials.

Meanwhile, his work was given more and more public exposure. He participated in approximately twenty group shows in several cities of Africa as well as in collective exhibitions in Lisbon (Portugal). His sculpture had such wide appeal that he was awarded a merit plaque.

José never lost his fascination for the native people - in particular the children. He was shocked that they had to work at such an early age when they should be protected by the family and go to school. It really hurt him to think that few had any future prospects. To illustrate this plight and to make

photo credit: Rev. C.L. Thompson

Boy Selling Wooden Toys medium: plaster painted in bronze patina dimensions: 70 cms

JOSE LOBO-FERNANDES

Tombazana medium: plaster

Football Player Charging Goalie 1973 medium: epoxy resin with mixed graphite and marble powder dimensions: width: 70 cms height: 39 cms An abstract highlighting body contact in the arena of sport, specifically soccer, players vying for possession of the ball

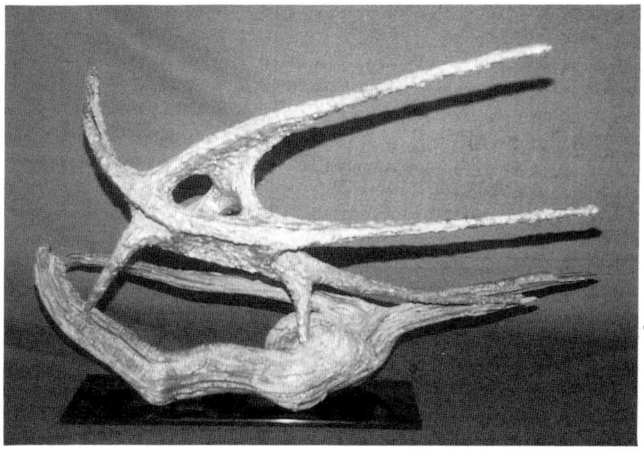

photo credit: Rev. C.L. Thompson

JOSE LOBO-FERNANDES

society aware of this shortcoming, he created several sculptures of those native boys, in rags, selling cheap wooden toys - secretly hoping that this might influence their future for the better.

Sometimes he even had to commute over enormous distances in Africa to do commissions such as the powerful group for a sports stadium, for instance, rhythmic movement expressed through body language. For one such project, he used a spraygun, filled it with wire that is crushed into very fine particles which, once released, end up forming a metal coating all over the sculpture.

His decoration of the Professional Centre of the Railways in Mozambique won him a bronze medal from the Government of Mozambique in recognition of his outstanding work.

For him, the energy and enthusiasm given to the creative moment is of essence, more so than the final product - it's what an artist gives to his work and what his work gives to him. He feels if an artist were too product-oriented, then it's no longer art but business.

Does he have any dream? Definitely so. He wants to create a environment within a translucent sculpture depicting movement, light and sound - his very own sculptural symphony. "It's only a dream," he comments, "but that's what keeps us humans alive; what gives us hope."

photo credit: Rev. C.L. Thompson

A. Schweitzer medium: cement fondu dimensions: 50 cms

Jose Lobo-Fernandes tremendously admires those who put their lives to a truly good purpose, pacifists such as Ghandhi, Martin Luther King, etc. and did this sculpture out of reverence for Albert Schweitzer whom he greatly respects.

DEBORAH LOUGHEED

Maybe this comment by Dr. D. Slaughter, doctor, art collector and writer, best sums up Deborah's unique talent:

..."Like most Canadian artists she is preoccupied with landscape but with a difference. Though she paints rural scenes of Ontario and Quebec, her strength stems from her unique paintings of the Rockies and the Foothills leading to them. Towering peaks (single panel) or whole mountain ranges (triptych) come alive in all their moods through her technique. As the natural light shifts, so do the colours of her palette, adding the feeling of motion to the scene...

"She achieves these remarkable effects, layering as many as seven coats of acrylic onto her panels, creating compacted memories of Alberta's distinctiveness..."

This exciting painter was born in Edmonton, Alberta. However, she has since lived in many cities across Canada and also in New York. She currently resides in Calgary and spends time in the mountains at the family cottage in Banff. She started painting at the age of four when she attended the Allied Art Centre in Calgary, and has been painting ever since.

Her work reaches beyond her native province. Her shows and exhibits span Canada (Edmonton, Calgary, Red Deer, Toronto, Hamilton, Kingston, etc. as well as smaller centers in Alberta through travelling exhibitions of the Alberta Society of Artists). The ASA is an association of professional artists, new members being selected by a Jury of the more senior artists. Deborah became a member in 1985 and has been involved in several of their group shows.

Award has followed upon award. For 1972-76 she was given the Imperial Oil Scholarship while attending Queen's University for her Fine Arts degree; in 1974, the Andre Bielier Award in Art and then, in 1979, the Banff School of Fine Arts Scholarship - her paintings being featured in over 50 public, corporate and private collections all around the country as well as in the United States of America and Australia.

This artist also made her mark by creating amazing mountain triptychs. These convey a feeling of greater space than single panels by emphasizing individual peaks as well as entire mountain

Meet Deborah LOUGHEED SINCLAIR, widely acclaimed painter whose work is regularly featured at the Kensington Gallery in Calgary, Alberta, and the Roberts Gallery in Toronto as well as in many group shows.

painting commissioned by Peter and Jeanne Lougheed after Kananaskis Provincial Park was renamed in the former Alberta Premier's honour

Lower Kananaskis Lake - Peter Lougheed Provincial Park medium: acrylic on canvas dimensions: 30 x 48 ins.

DEBORAH LOUGHEED

Victoria Glacier - Lake Louise Triptych in the collection of Home Oil Company Limited medium: acrylic on canvas 3 panels each dimensions: 30 x 24 ins.

The centre panel was featured in the February 1989 issue of Key to Calgary declaring Deborah Lougheed Sinclair the Artist of the Month.

"Deborah is very much a local artist," observes Janny Hutchinson of Kensington/Paperworks Galleries. "Her work typifies what we see in the mountains, in our very own landscape - what we live with. She brings it to life."

ranges. They are powerful visual documentaries with special emphasis on light, colour, texture, dramatic spatial tension drawing the beholder right into her very artwork rather than creating the effect of viewing from afar. A large triptych of Nakiska - site of the Calgary Winter Olympic Games - was recently commissioned for the new Amoco Center in Calgary.

Most of her paintings are later completed in detail from ten-to-fifteen minute sketches she does on location with the media she has on hand at that moment, the main emphasis being placed on colour and feeling. Only later (in small acrylic-on-paper preliminary studies) does she pay particular attention to composition and detail and to the exact colour relationships. She uses felt pen and water colour for special effect in preliminary sketches but never applies too much technique for fear of impairing the natural fluency. However, essentially there does remain a relationship between those preliminary sketches and the final paintings. Lately, she has also been using water-soluble coloured pencils for their ease of handling - as well as for the limited space and weight taken for hiking. Occasionally she also paints from photographs taken for special memory storage, such as striking light conditions. Her husband, a medical researcher, and their three children share with her all those wonderful experiences of trips to different parts of Canada for sketching and some hiking.

Since 1976 Deborah has worked almost exclusively in acrylics. She applies, first of all, an underpainting with opaque colours. She then mixes the paint with a thick acrylic gel medium that becomes clear when it dries. Many transparent and semi-transparent layers are used in completing the paintings, the proportion of gel to paint being a critical factor. Her transparent layers allow the impression of suffused settings reflecting the particular mood of the season or day, like the sun breaking through a crisp background.

Prior to acrylics, Deborah worked in oil and did sculpture and printmaking. She considered her studies at Queen's from 1972 to 1976, a good time for experimenting with different disciplines until she finally realized that acrylic paint gave her the tool to best express her vision of the Canadian landscape.

In 1984 an exhibition and art purchase programme was initiated, as a memorial to the deceased Thomas James Scurfield, to stimulate interest in the Sunshine area in Banff National Park. From 150 entries, a select exhibition of 23 works was chosen for display at the Banff Centre. Deborah's work, GREAT WHITE WAY, SUNSHINE, featuring only off-white, lilac and bluish pastel tints, was chosen at this First Exhibition, not only for the show and to be purchased, but also for the Special Purchase Award.

Oesa Trail - Lake Victoria painting from Deborah's Lake O'Hara series medium: acrylic on canvas dimensions: 30 x 42 ins.

This painting was chosen for the 1989 - 1990 Glenbow Museum Acquisitions Society Seventh Annual Art Lotto. Deborah fully supports this fundraising because it serves a very worthwhile cause while generating good publicity at the same time.

There couldn't be a better way to describe Deborah, one of their members, than that offered by the Alberta Society of Artists based on the artist's vision of her work:

"...Deborah portrays the Canadian landscape in a representational style based on strong underlying abstract principles. The everchanging mood of the land is depicted primarily through colour, both subtle and dramatic. Her vision of the Canadian landscape juxtaposes the permanence of the land itself against transitions of colour, light, texture, and rhythm most evident in nature's changing seasons. These expressions of the land are attained with the layering of transparent acrylic paint over an opaque underpainting..."

The C.S.P.G. (CANADIAN SOCIETY OF PETROLEUM GEOLOGISTS) sponsored an open house for artists so that they could learn about geology and the world around them. The artists were then invited to submit proposals for major work, applying what they had learned. The Show was called "Exploring the Earth Through Art."

The C.S.P.G. next selected thirty artists from over one hundred, to do a multi-panel for an exhibition the following year. Deborah did a triptych of the Athabasca Glacier. Deborah's triptych was purchased by an M. Tremblay of Calgary. This painting was chosen for the 1989-90 Glenbow Museum Acquisitions Society Seventh Annual ART LOTTO.

Deborah, who had a solo show entitled ALONG MOUNTAIN TRAILS - Lake O'Hara (just on the far side of the Continental Divide), spent many trips hiking, sketching and taking photographs in this area from June until late September when the larch were turning.

This time, she used more photographs than usual because some of the hikes took up a good part of the day just getting there and left less time for sketching. However, she relied mainly on the expe-

Springback Farm medium: acrylic on canvas dimensions: 24 x 30 ins.

DEBORAH LOUGHEED

Wenkchemna Peaks - Valley of the Ten Peaks medium: acrylic on canvas dimension: 30 x 36 ins.

riences and visual memories of these hikes to convey the particular mood and character of each painting, for each day and each hike in the Lake O'Hara area are indelibly etched into her memory.

The ALONG MOUNTAIN TRAILS show featured 16 large canvases. Three of these were multi-panel ones: two triptychs and one polytych (4 panels). The exhibition, furthermore, included 16 works on paper that were her working studies for the series.

In 1989, this artist was selected to do a commission for Canadian Airlines International for reproduction as Calgary's destination poster. The painting was to depict Calgary with the mountains and also some form of human activity.

This marks the first time that Deborah added figures to her painting - something quite unusual - but a most challenging and satisfying experience. Her painting "Along the Bow" depicts the Bow River and three cyclists. The posters came out that September and can be seen at some travel agents or Canadian Airlines offices.

JIRINA MARTON

Meet Jirina MARTON, graphic designer and children's book illustrator whose work has been acclaimed worldwide.

Multilingual Jirina MARTON (nee KAKUBUV), feeling fully at ease in Czech, French, Italian and English, was born on April 19th, 1946, in Liberec (Czechoslovakia) where her mother was an opera singer. The family moved to Prague when Jirina was five.

She was an extremely sensitive child. At the mere age of three she would experience blissful happiness just by lying in the grass on a sunny day underneath a tree, watching its leaves rustle in the wind.

Jirina was about four years old when she engaged in her first major "Artistic venture." Her mother was painting the kitchen and - much to her mother's dismay - Jirina had the exciting idea of contributing her share by decorating a complete wall. Of course, her mother was not exactly enraptured with her daughter's artistic enthusiasms and

Untitled children's book illustration
medium: acrylics dimensions: 275 x 342 mm

JIRINA MARTON

Untitled illustration for children's book called Mitzi
medium: acrylics dimensions: 552 x 342 mm

Untitled children's book illustration
medium: acrylics dimensions: 276 x 342 mm

repainted the entire surface.

While at elementary school, Jirina did many small drawings. Everyone always wanted them and that proved to be a great incentive. Then, when Jirina turned fourteen, her art instructor warmly recommended that she attend an art school with a four-year programme where she did wood sculpture. After that, she tried almost any kind of work for - as she explains - people in East European countries have to work - no matter what. Otherwise one would be considered as living off the work of others which is deemed criminal and, consequently, she gave up painting for quite some time. When she left her homeland it was like leaving her old nature behind, totally erasing her past. Yet she did not feel sad at all because it was her explicit and cherished decision to leave - without any regrets - in order to turn over a new leaf.

She was blessed with talent, but unfortunately, lacked perseverance until she met a friend who truly encouraged her. From then on she really dedicated herself to painting. As she needed absolute artistic freedom, she decided to leave for France and settled in Paris for a period of seven years where she started a career as children's book illustrator.

In order to supplement her income, she worked for approximately five months with the painter AGAM who specializes in kinetic art with superimposed designs - artwork in motion that changes form depending on one's angle of viewing - creating the most amazing effects.

JIRINA MARTON

Untitled children's book illustration

By the time she was given a chance to immigrate to the United States, she had become emotionally involved and it was simply impossible for her to tear herself away from Paris.

Jirina subsequently worked as layout artist for the Larousse Publishing House and, at the same time, also did children's book illustrations. She had always had a great knack for easily establishing contact with children. She finds them truly fascinating, all the more so since - very much to her regret - being so fond of children, she could never have a child of her own. She, therefore, felt like populating their world with her designs. She could put herself in their shoes and see everything from their angle. She always reads her stories to them and shows them her designs while critically studying their little faces for their reaction. They never hold back but come straight out with their comments. All the drawing she formally studied and formerly knew, she now has to "forget." Instead, she places herself in the position of a small child who creates instinctively without knowing anything about art - painting things as she feels them. She creates spontaneously because she feels that pure intellect hampers the flow of creativity and can even destroy it.

Her love for children, her understanding of them and her touching illustrations were soon crowned by success. Her books were published in Switzerland, France, Japan and one book featuring her illustrations, NICOLE'S BOAT, was published in Canada by Annick Press Ltd. This was followed by MIDNIGHT VISIT IN MOLLY'S HOUSE (by the same publisher) for which Jirina also wrote the text.

Jirina has been living in Canada now for three

JIRINA MARTON

years and finally the miracle happened - she was blessed with a child of her own - her daughter, Michelle. She finds it wonderful to have her own child and watch her every move and reaction. Little Michelle, who is the joy of Jirina's life and her reason for living, gives her much inspiration, so much so that she manages to keep up her work as illustrator. She banishes any worries by listening to good music. Jirina has always enjoyed music, particularly operas, since she was raised in that milieu which she finds very soothing.

Personally, Jirina is a very modest person who hardly talks about her work but lets her hands do all the talking. Her work does, indeed, speak for itself.

Untitled children's book illustration medium: acrylics dimensions: 276 x 342 mm

LOU POLLOCK

photo by Ken Bell

Meet Lou POLLOCK, one of Canada's native daughters of Ojibway descent, a talented writer with a strong message and a painter of great sensitivity - having worked as reporter for a daily paper and, in a volunteer capacity, for the late Lester B. Pearson.

Having willed her children wings to fly, Lou now lives on her own, dedicating most of her time to writing, sketching, painting, and embroidery; preserving her native culture in outline and design.

She was stirred into writing - an outpouring of her soul - by very deeply moving experiences and she writes best when angry or in despair.

Lou's ideas and inspirations stem from a well-founded philosophy. Her view of life was bequeathed to her by her mother, an Indian midwife, who went to see her patients by canoe during the summer and - in winter - by horse and cutter. This wise woman was forever witnessing the cycles of life and death - yet always cheerful. It was she who taught her daughter how to serve others and how to respect and protect the environment.

Stemming from a background of deeply spiritual native religion, the concern for the survival of our habitat took a strong hold of this artist. She suddenly felt the urge to illustrate her poetry. She also thought that people not familiar with her culture, might not immediately understand her way of seeing things. Graphic representation renders ideas and concepts easily intelligible and accessible. It even helps to reinforce expressed ideas. Thus, since the Seventies, Lou has been complementing her writing with illustrations.

Apart from her fantastic pencil sketches, done on the spur of the moment, Lou has also been experimenting with acrylics. Her painting of the SEA IN TURMOIL leaves a special impact on the viewer. It is alive with movement. You can practically feel the churning of the sea. Yet her artwork is very structured. Lou knows how to delicately balance realistic elements and artistic content.

However, this artist prefers to work in pen and ink. With this medium, her thoughts quickly flow onto the paper while the ideas are still fresh in her mind. She is not very patient by nature and likes to do everything fast, but - she is also at her best when working speedily.

Eagle medium: pen and ink dimensions: 12 x 9 in.

LOU POLLOCK

One of the symbols recurring over and over again in all her work, is the eagle (featured in the national emblem of several countries) - symbol of almost godlike power. The eagle overlooks everything but when the environment kills Brother Eagle then mankind, too, is doomed to perish - for a polluted world is unfit for survival.

This pressing concern for the environment is powerfully depicted in THE AGONY OF THE GREAT EAGLE - wings wide spread and head thrust back imploring the Creator for protection, for salvation from mankind's self-inflicted ruin.

THE AGONY OF THE GREAT EAGLE

The Great Eagle cries
his last cry
agonized at what he sees
brother fighting brother
destruction
from sea to sea
bombs of unbelievable power
blood flowing, churning,
children running--running
nowhere to flee

the Eagle kneels before his Creator
begging for one more chance
to alert his brothers
to dance the warrior's dance
they will battle the enemies of nature
and bind her bleeding wounds
their screams will penetrate
the walls of apathy
for understanding
must come soon. . .

listen...to the cry of the Great Eagle
walk softly through the woods
seek him high above the tree tops
a weary, battered warrior
crying to be understood
listen...to his cry
wash acid from the raindrops
take the scientist with his brain
show him how to crown his glory
with happiness. . .not pain

Lou sees that the water near her hometown is so polluted you can almost walk on it and it smells like rotten eggs. Indians like to go fishing but can no longer enjoy eating their catch due to mercury contamination - not even brought about by their own race, but by the white man.

Lou's mother would often take her children by canoe. If anyone ever dropped a papercover or chocolate wrapper carelessly or unintentionally into the water she would turn around trying to retrieve it. She would tell her children NEVER TO OFFEND THE SPIRIT OF THE WATER. "Never date using water as a waste dump for one day your life may depend on it."

Lou is 65 years old and still at the height of her creative energy. She lets her poetry flow freely from her subconscious - poetry with a special spark that touches all of us, makes us wonder and - identify.

Mother Teaching Her Child How To Do Basket Weaving medium: acrylic dimensions: 10 x 8 ins.

photo by Ken Bell

LOU POLLOCK

Before I go
Oh Lord let me have
one more fling
from the branch
of the sensual tree

I want to feel the tingle
of fingers entwined
of a sudden hug
of a far away glance
meeting mine

I want to feel
the cascade of power
the knowing
I can melt a frown
with a smile

I want to feel
every cell in my body
come alive

I want to laugh
in the deepest dark of night
and delve into secrets
only we can know

I want to once again
feel for one hour
the complete melding
of thought, body and soul in nature's
pinnacle of emotional glow
one hour lord...
before I go...

This poem, which was first published in COMPANION (July/August 1985 issue), won Lou The SPIRES First Prize for the PHILOSOPHY OF LIFE category.

Her poems were also featured in COMPASS and ELDERS.

Her genuine concerns are reflected in many poems such as BROKEN PADDLE (publ. in COMPANION - Sept. 1984 issue) excerpt:

...What shell I tell my father?
I tried to hold back the flying monsters
who sprayed our forests with death
I tried to hold back the waters
that carried mercury silver in our nets.

photo by Ken Bell

Protect My Brother medium: pencil sketch dimensions: 10 x 7 ins.

This artist's achievement is all the more admirable since she has been painting only since 1965 and never actually underwent any formal training, but is truly self-taught.

Lou is extremely fond of children, the mother and child motif being another theme constantly recurring in her artwork. Another frequent emphasis is the mother as teacher, since Lou is also keenly interested in EDUCATION, a field close to her heart. She illustrates this theme with but a few strokes. There are not unnecessary items whatsoever. She uses a bare minimum of depiction, creating impact with astonishing economy stressing simplicity of lines such as shown in MOTHER TEACHING HER CHILD HOW TO DO BASKET WEAVING.

Lou, who was brought up as a Catholic focuses her belief in God, rather than in the religious institution per se. She takes great interest in all current issues. When the Pope, whom she calls the Fisherman, came for a visit to Canada, she did highly symbolistic drawings such as depicting the Pope walking past the Canadian native people - in the splendour of ritual - but without truly identifying with their problems and concerns.

She is a strong woman who lives by her convictions and never compromises on her values. She

LOU POLLOCK

Elder Surrounded By Eagerly Listening Children medium: pen and ink dimensions 10 x 8 ins.

is, for instance, totally opposed to the spraying of pesticides and weed killers, particularly since so many people are suffering from allergies.

One day she looked out to see a civic employee who was about to spray her daughter's lawn for weeds. She confronted him and asked him to skip their property because her grandson suffers from asthma, promising him she would personally pull out the weeds. A short while later when she looked out of the window, she was astonished to find that he had totally ignored her plea and was busy spraying. Yes, Lou is a woman who meets any confrontation head-on. She simply can't understand how some people can be so insensitive towards nature and their fellow-humans.

What are Lou's dreams for the future? Perhaps to return to the small village in Northern Ontario where she was raised and where she has a total identification with nature.

PASSIONARIA SECKA

Meet Passionaria SECKA, this unique blend of jewellery, consumer goods and industrial designer, muralist, pastel painter and sculptor.

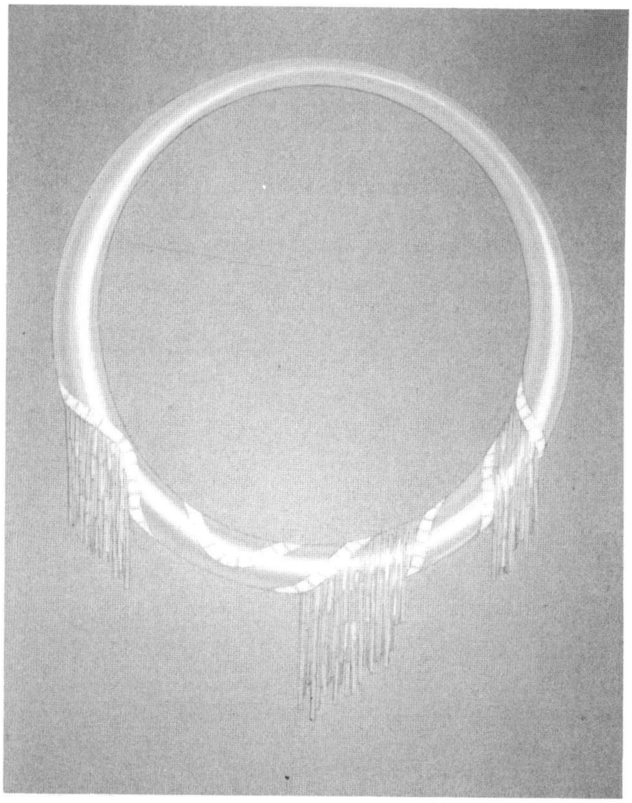

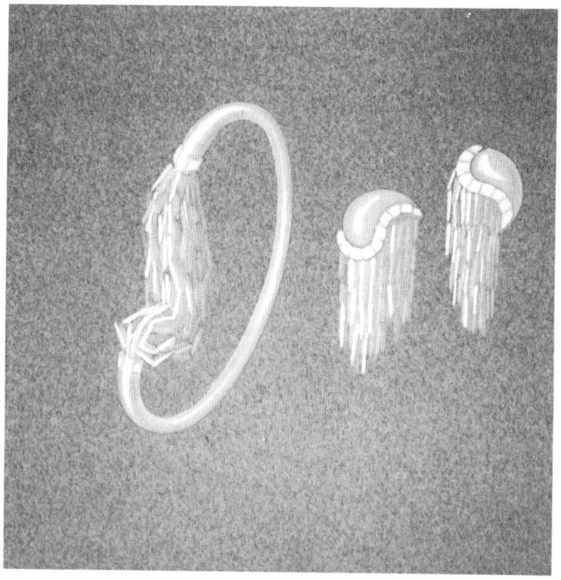

Set of gold necklace, bangle and earrings high-lighted by diamonds (standard size)

PASSIONARIA SECKA

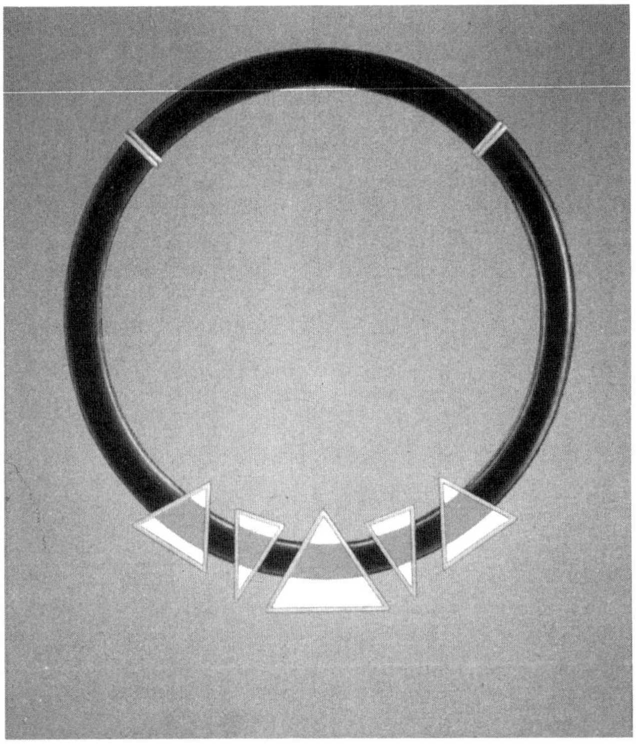

Jewellery set of black coral (or onyx) highlighted by red and white enamel

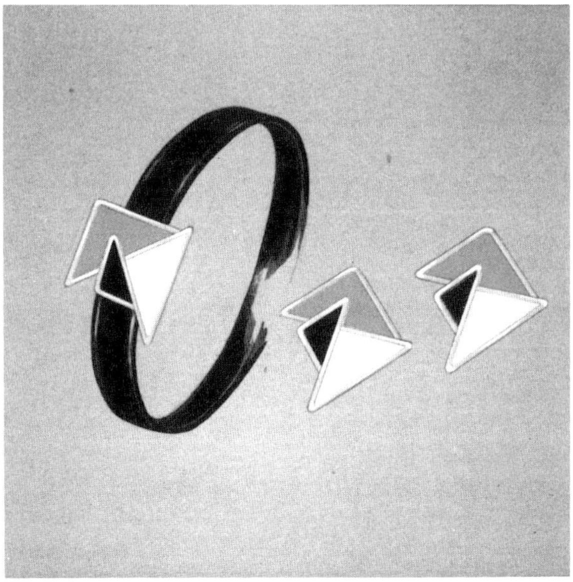

Passionaria was born on August 19th, 1947, in Bulgaria. Her father, who was very fond of art and rather talented with his hands, soon realized his daughter's artistic inclinations and skills. He supported her in all her endeavors.

As a little girl she very much enjoyed drawing - especially with colours - and while still attending elementary school also vigorously pursued a sculpting course for children. She was so talented that at the mere age of ten (10) she participated in her first exhibition featuring animal sculptures.

In high school, her interests slightly shifted and she became fascinated with ceramics, concentrating on decorating ceramics and glass - this being part of a four-year programme of specialization. She completed her secondary education in 1966.

She then moved to Prague where she enrolled with the University of Applied Arts, School of Industrial Design, for a period of six years, studying industrial design from 1966 to 1972. The first year was more of a general course with emphasis on charcoal drawing and sculptures - and plenty of theory - whereas the fifth year was almost exclusively dedicated to industrial design. The sixth-year course the graduation year emphasized the students' creation of their own work samples.

Those formative years in Prague were highly important for her artistic growth but also took on a quite different, special personal significance. It was at the School of Industrial Design that Passionaria met her husband who was studying the same discipline. She was two years his senior in studies. They shared many common interests and soon got married without either of them knowing that, even professionally, many joint future projects would closely bind them together.

From 1972 to 1975 Passionaria then enrolled with the Institute of Industrial Design in Sofia, Bulgaria, a country where she worked as a freelance designer.

All of a sudden, she developed a special interest in jewellery design, being completely self-taught in that field, creating truly unique and aesthetically pleasing designs.

Her stunningly impressive jewellery with unusual decorative motifs is extremely versatile. It can be elegantly executed not only in precious metals but also in synthetic materials. Thus it warrants an easy adaptation to contemporary costume jewellery that is in vogue and in great demand today since it is fairly inexpensive and thus widely affordable.

In Bulgaria precious metals are relatively scarce and fairly costly. Even silver can't be obtained in large quantities without some problems, yet Passionaria designed mainly in silver. The appeal of her work was such that all her creations sold the moment she had finished them.

She designs in keeping with contemporary trends but is - at the same time - extremely fond of antique jewellery which she conceptually transforms, thereby adapting it to modern application. Generally, however, her designs are the brainchildren of her own creative mind combined with modern influences.

Yet her fascination goes far beyond jewellery design. She is interested in the harmony of plastic design, a universal discipline that teaches good taste regarding our environment and how to bring about improvement through design. Looking back at her professional training, Passionaria comments: "The path each graduate follows is completely left up to the individual. Some of my classmates went on to design ships, others designed industrial plants - but all of us found fulfillment and success."

Her consumer goods range from the chromatically extremely appealing, highly functional toys

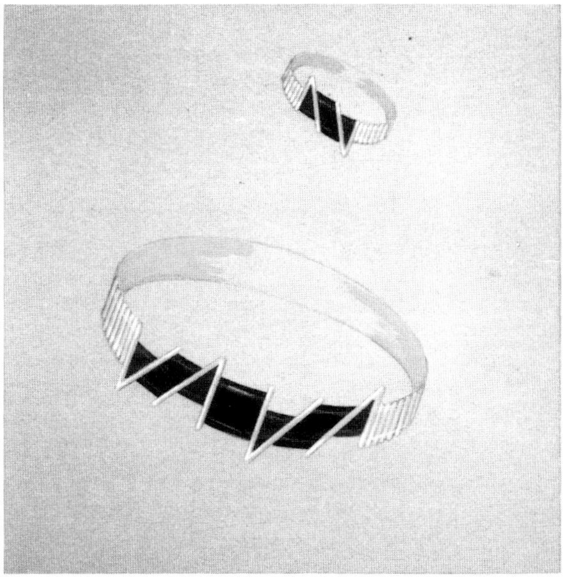

Jewellery set (precious metals) gold, lepis lazuli, black onyx, diamonds

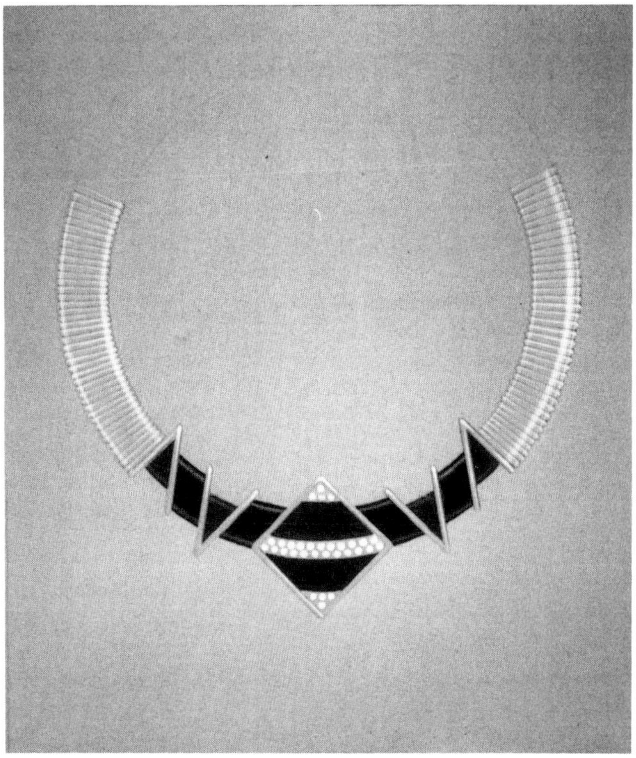

PASSIONARIA SECKA

Mural - Children's swimming pool in Brno medium: sheets of metal sprayed with epoxy paint dimensions: 9 x 5 m

for children such as rattles, tops, clocks, etc. that exude a truly cheerful attraction, to graphic and interior decorations, climaxing in the highly challenging design of entire technical facilities. In that last mentioned specialty, Passionaria contributed, for instance, to a Tractor Manufacturing Plant - a project executed by her husband.

Yet her talent reaches even beyond that. She has also created murals for a children's swimming pool in Brmo and still does sculptures. However, these latter are strictly for her own pleasure and very personal enjoyment.

Passionaria, who had several exhibitions in Bulgaria, Czechoslovakia and Austria, is now dreaming about the possibility of continuing her profession - preferably designing jewellery. She hopes to thereby contribute to Canada, her new homeland.

Meanwhile, her most cherished desire came true. She is now working as a designer for D'Orlan Jewellers who design and produce jewellery for Nina Ricci in Paris.

ARNO SOLTESZ

Meet Arno SOLTESZ, a versatile artist whose repertoire spans painting, graphics, murals, stained glass work of brilliant colouring and rhythmic lines, custom-made gold jewellery of rare craftsmanship, furniture design, interior design and striking, painstakingly finished ceramics of most unusual delicacy and perfection of form, a poet and linguist who feels equally comfortable in Hungarian, Czech, German, Russian, French, and English.

Arno SOLTESZ was born in Hungary during the Second World War. At the mere age of seven he already showed such promise that his parents - despite some financial hardship - provided him with private classes in woodworking and metalwork. His instructor was extremely strict. He was bent on bringing out the best in his students. It was he who impressed upon Arno the importance of fine drawing skills and flawless craftsmanship.

Arno's hometown was annexed by Czechoslovakia. In 1956, his mind was constantly bombarded by radio appeals from Freedom Fighters of the Hungarian uprising. These set his poetic mind aflame and gave him such a strong yearning for Freedom that he tried to cross the border into Hungary together with a few classmates. He was caught. His fervent patriotism landed him in a Correctional Camp where he was settled with an eight-month sentence. Being of an indomitable spirit, Arno tried to make the best of his experience. Making clay portraits of fellow inmates and the guards he concentrated on raising some money on the side. Yet, although he derived personal satisfaction from his artistic endeavors, money did not bring him any happiness at this stage. Instead, he ended up in Solitary Confinement. Once his sentence was served, Arno went back to high school, devoting as much time as possible to art.

Simultaneously, he also combined his talent for unique design with the well-founded technical skills of his brother, a jeweller. He taught Arno the shaping of precious metals, mould-making and lost wax casting, a learning experience that would prove highly valuable to him decades later.

Next, Arno was drafted for two years into the Czechoslovak People's Army. Upon completion of the compulsory military service, he enrolled with the Fine Arts School in Bratislava. There he studied Classical and Byzantine Art for two and a half years. Suddenly, Fate smiled on him. He was chosen to visit France on a cultural exchange.

It had not been all that easy for Arno to leave art school. But how was he to resist the west with its artistic freedom! His eyes light up when he talks

ARNO SOLTESZ

about Paris - the city of lights that breathes art. He was simply overwhelmed by the high quality of the artwork - frescoes and murals - truly monumental works.

Eventually, he was given asylum in France. He served in the French Foreign Legion. Wounded, he spent his recovery sketching portraits. A new avenue opened up to him. He became a tourist painter until enticed to the New World in 1970 by curiosity to explore and - the love of a lady who was living in Canada.

He now dedicated himself to art, doing some advertising graphics and other freelance artwork, whenever available. As soon as his funds would dwindle, he worked either in construction or as a security guard in order to defray the daily expenses - always keeping his dignity as man, the provider.

Then, in 1973, Arno participated in the Cinquième Concours de la Palme d'Or des Baux-Arts, held in Monte Carlo, Monaco. He was represented in this Competition with two works, one titled GUARD - a design executed in India ink - and the other, HEAD OF SOLDIER, an etching in mixed techniques.

Arno found it next to impossible to live exclusively off his income derived from art. Although he sold his artwork overseas where it fetched him rather high prices, some people are just not born to be artist and businessman all at once.

His life had its ups and downs. When the going was tough, Arno's humour would come to the forefront in his poetry:

FOR SALE
ONE UNSUNG SONG
NEEDLESSLY LONG
ONE USELESS VIOLIN
SPIDERS ARE NESTING IN.
Also:
ONE DEBASED LIFE
FEW BROKEN DREAMS
FEW UNSHED TEARS
ASSORTED FEARS
ONE RUSTED PENKNIFE.
ANYONE? PLEASE!

Dec. 16th, 1984.

One-Rose Vases sizes ranging from 27 to 32 cms 1986-1987 medium: clay

By the time the Spring of 1985 approached, Arno - despite all his optimism - could not even remotely imagine a promising future. Yet Fate knew better. When taking a stroll one day along Black Creek in northern Toronto, Arno came across rich yellow clay. He gathered some and automatically started kneading it. Suddenly the light dawned. That was it! Ceramics - the answer to his problems! He no longer wasted time. Oh, how his hands were crying out for ceramics! How could he have ignored his calling for so long!

Now, how would he be able to afford a potter's wheel, tools and a kiln? Initially, a store fired his work - piece by piece - but gradually Arno converted the family livingroom into a studio, using any utensils within his reach, as tools.

Next, he immersed himself in modelling in order to perfect his skills. He also added decorative finishing. On the other hand, he also became aware that working with purchased dry greenware had its own share of problems, as pieces would frequently break on firing.

But Arno is no quitter. Yet once the aspect of temperature control was mastered, another problem arose. He simply could not get used to greenware forms and shapes. The artist within him rebelled. Premoulded greenware just did not fit his idea of art. If only he could handcraft it! It suddenly dawned on him that the joining of two greenware

ARNO SOLTESZ

Decorative vessel with Latin prayer and copper rings
medium: clay dimensions 48 cm 1987

clamshell halves would result in a hollow product. Then, he would join the vertical halves while manually forming a base, neck, and stopper. Now he was able to form hollow flasks and decanters as well as vases, having circumvented the need for a potter's wheel.

However, there still remained the problem of colour. Arno started to fervently experiment till he found his solution - a non-toxic finish with stunning colourings. Next, he took a careful look at metallic glazing. Again he explored until he found an aesthetically pleasing, safe and durable lustre. He now combined the outer sheen with a soft-colour interior, highlighting the pleasing gentle hues of the liquid.

Being extremely talented, Arno did not stop here. He finally succeeded in getting moulded greenware in the wet stage granting him greater flexibility of his handcrafted modifications. Besides, the stone setting skills acquired from his brother, now proved to be a valuable asset leading to metal embedding techniques. His decorating repertoire presently includes metal band inserts as well as precious metal and gemstone inlays.

Some of his extremely appealing art objects take hundreds of hours to create and perfect, and feature silver, gold and gemstone inlays.

This artist's designs are so distinctive that there are no two objects completely alike. The ornamentation alone is a pleasure to behold featuring an understated elegance despite a certain degree of opulence.

To Arno, functionality and aesthetic delight must go hand in hand. He feels a noble beverage deserves a matching vessel that can be familiar and classical all at once - as far removed from serialization as possible. Just as each wine has its own distinctive bouquet, so each decanter should have its own grace of form and uniqueness of texture and colouring.

Here, in Canada, a truly personalized elitist tradition could develop using ceramic chalices that have the names of family members or the family crest engraved.

In November 1988, the artist held a Ceramic Exhibition at the Laurier Gallery in Toronto's west-end. I had the opportunity to ask him what really

ARNO SOLTESZ

Vases - incised design medium: clay dimensions: 30 and 27 cms respectively 1987

mattered to him in life and, without a moment's hesitation, he promptly replied: "To do art, and most importantly in my art, to totally project myself into it, preserving honesty and purity, for art never suffers any pretention and definitely no cliches." Being creative, Arno breathes life into the clay, imprinting his own expression.

Arno, who is endowed with penetrating perception and great sensitivity, has an innate feeling for colour, the beauty and grace of form and fluency of line.

Many of his most recent creations inspire a uniquely archaeological feeling. Some feature gods of mythology. Others show human figures or Latin inscriptions taken from Christian writings. His jugs, in particular, transpose the beholder into the Biblical Age conjuring visions of Canaa, for instance. Sometimes he uses his vessels and containers to tell entire stories.

Lately, Arno has further diversified by creating portable room dividers with mosaic inlay, some of them depicting religious motifs.

Arno does indeed take great pride in quality and he only applies his seal once he is satisfied with the flawless nature of his artwork. People who formerly never much cared for ceramics, have already turned into avid collectors of his work.

Symbols slab glass wall design for new church in Rochester, NY, USA dimensions: 23 x 9 x 2 ft.

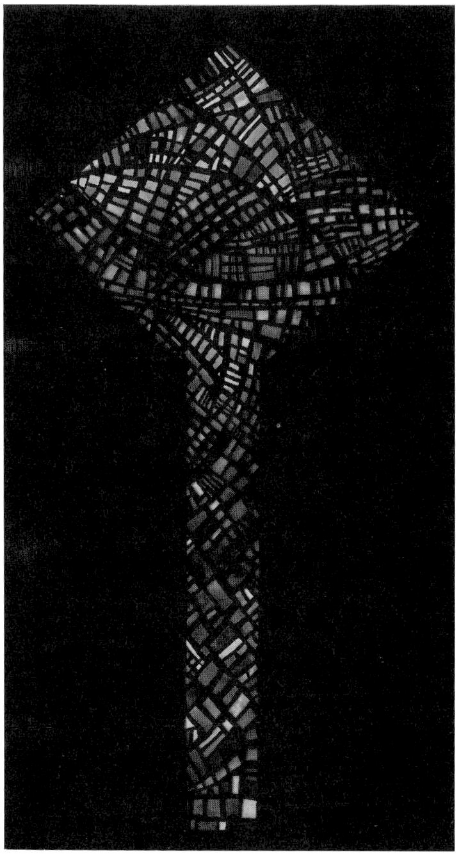

MARGARET SPATARU

Meet Margaret SPATARU, predominantly a mural painter being a woman of varied talents constantly exploring all the facets of the arts such as acrylics, oil, silkscreen, pen and ink as well as life drawings.

The Night

The Night pen and ink on paper 32 x 26 ins. 1980

Already at the age of six, Margaret SPATARU - born in Roumania - was well known in her school for her artistic talent and admired for her crystal-clear, unfaltering decision to become an artist. Yes, even as a child she knew beyond the slightest shadow of a doubt that there was only one course clearly charted for her - that of an artist. During her childhood, she was simultaneously inclined towards art and literature, excelling in both fields, publishing poetry and having art exhibitions.

At high school, she took academics and, in addition, whole-heartedly enjoyed doing piano compositions, acting and ballet.

Prior to the completion of her high school studies, she had a first exhibition with 180 pieces of artwork. This was televised all over Roumania. Besides, her work was written up in several art magazines and other publications. (1972 - "One-Woman Show" - exhibition presented at the "Institute of Creative Arts and Design" in Bucharest, Roumania).

She then enrolled with the University of Fine Arts in Bucharest where she combined arts and academics and, while at the university, participated in several university-sponsored group exhibitions. The artists would work at a retreat in the country and then hold exhibitions at the rate of four per year.

In those days, Professor Gheorge SARU was her spiritual mentor, influencing her in her thinking in art but giving her total freedom to develop her own style. In her paintings, she is inclined to ex-

MARGARET SPATARU

press inner atmospheres and spiritual adventures and, in this respect, relates to the metaphysical Belgian surrealist, Paul DELVAUX. This artist, in an almost inconspicuously skillful manner, blends the conventional with the unexpected - such as female nudes against a backdrop of traditional buildings in a totally natural setting. He leaves it to the viewers to read into it whatever they please without providing any explanation whatsoever. Somehow this juxtaposition of unexpected effects - subconscious significance conjured by chance imagery - really intrigues this artist.

During the year of her graduation, Margaret had another "One Woman Show" - an exhibition of oil paintings at the "Roumanian Atheneum Gallery" in Bucharest, Roumania.

In 1976 she then graduated from the University of Fine Arts, Painting Department, with a Master's Degree, and a rating of ten - the highest grade attainable - having majored in painting, drawing, artistic anatomy, perspective drawing, various techniques, and art history. In 1977, she had another "One Woman Show" featuring oil paintings, decorative art and graphic art at the Sirius Gallery in Sibiu, Roumania. She then spent two years touring Denmark, Greece and Israel where galleries and private collectors purchased her artwork.

The Dreamer

The Dreamer pen & ink on paper 32 x 26 ins. 1980

During the first year in Canada she designed the scenery for "Three Folk Tales", a televised theatrical event presented in Spring by the "Blessed Marguerite Bourgeoys School" in Scarborough. Then, she participated for two years in a row in the Annual Multicultural Fine Arts Exhibition, held at the O'Keefe Centre for the Performing Arts in Toronto.

In 1982 she participated in a group show at the "St. Lawrence Theatre," followed by a "One Woman Show" at Gallery 76. In 1983, Margaret SPATARU graduated from the Ontario College of Art (OCA), Experimental Arts Department. She also showed in the OCA "Open House" exhibition. During that year, on the occasion of the Inaugural Banquet for the opening of the Airway Centre No. II (Toronto) built by Inducon, she also participated in a one-woman art display featuring 80 of her paintings. As well she took part in the International Symposium Cantacusino in Vienna, Austria. In-between she had four of her pen and ink compositions lithographed and some of her artwork was sold to the Italian Institute of Culture, the Columbus Centre.

In 1984, she was commissioned the design and painting of the mural for NABISCO BRANDS (Christie Brown division) for their main lobby opening up to the executive suites. (Dimensions: 21' x 14'.) This mural is done in coloured greys and is entitled ARCTIC TRANQUILLITY. NABISCO also presented posters of the mural for their annual Christmas promotion and displayed same (approx. 40,000) all over Canada and the United States. In 1984, she also participated in the Annual Group Exhibition at the Toronto "Central Hospital"; in 1985, at the Alliance Française and, in 1987, in the Roumanian Exhibition at the Prestigious Roberts Gallery Limited. Next, she won a competition for a 15'x 8' mural based on a Turkish rock scenery. This was for the lobby of the Oshawa Medical Clinic, a seven-story building located downtown on King Street.

Margaret was always considered a colourist.

MARGARET SPATARU

Her original technique monoprints are quite successful in New York and Toronto where some of them were purchased by IBM and other institutions.

Why did Margaret - after a span of approximately fifteen years - leave figurative painting behind and switch to abstract painting? She had reached the point where she felt the need for breaking conventional barriers. She was driven by a strong urge to say more than merely expressing herself in figurative images. She started expressing the abstract in abstract ways, commenting; "I could no longer express abstract thoughts in existing words and terms." The abstract became her element, since it does not limit imagination. "There is a whole abstract world within each of us, but you can reach only as far as your own depth of thinking.

"An empty abstract, loosely thrown together, may mean absolutely nothing and convey no other feelings to the viewer than a sense of decorativeness, but - if the reason behind it is the necessity to communicate the inner feelings by bringing the world within out into the light in its pure abstract state without translating it into figurative expression - then the artwork offers depth, identification and delight.

"The abstract process should not be confused by the stylization process which starts from reality by eliminating the unnecessary details that do not add to the definition keeping only those details defining the essence, not the descriptiveness.

The abstractionist knowingly eliminates the figurative images while preserving the concept. Where there is a very deep meaning to be sensed, abstract artwork will definitely move the beholder's state of mind.

Her natural tendencies for colours and expressions of inner life are represented best by an abstract style where there are no barriers to dreams and representation. But in academic drawing, figurative style and life drawing she is also very much at home. She sees each composition in monumental sizes which explains her main interest and her capability of coping with murals. Classical music is inspiring her while painting. Travelling and experiencing beauty, together with the folklore of the different countries, are strong needs along with the one for painting.

After the response from her exhibition in New York, Margaret wanted to make her artwork available for public viewing and opened her own studio gallery, ART STUDIO "M", at 35 Briar Hill Avenue, on the 2nd floor.

Genesis 10 - detail 54 x 42 ins mixed technique on canvas 1989

What are her dreams for the immediate future? To do as many murals as possible for private residences and shopping malls, for all to see and enjoy.

MARGARET SPATARU

Mural for a private residence medium: acrylic on wall dimensions: 17 x 8 ft.

HARRY TANNER

Meet Harry TANNER, whose paintings are of compelling intensity and powerfully wide grassroot appeal. They sear an indelible imprint in your mind, making you eager to find out more about the artist/ work-of-art interrelationship. HERE HE IS, a truly unique artist who, with touching warmth and humility, spontaneously gives credit to those encouraging him.

Entering his studio, your senses are bombarded by a great diversity of work talking straight to you, stirring you into reflection and confrontation about the underlying meaning.

You can feast your eyes on stunning Toronto cityscapes such as the Eaton Centre and a bus stop, or a girl's portrait, the artist struggling in a snowstorm - extremely realistic in their dimensions and yet creating a reality all their own. As Harry Tanner remarks: "You simply cannot copy reality unless in photography. It is the combined architectural and human significance that matters."

In this work "Self-Portrait in Toronto", the storm is indicated by swirls - the discontinued invisible lines of the swirls being in strict adherence to the ancient law of Greek composition.

Tanner also does socio-historical paintings, such as the full-size portrait of POUNDMAKER, a Canadian hero, a Cree Blackfoot Indian who - during the Louis Riel uprising - fought the whiteman and won.

This artist (initially self-taught) has been painting ever since his childhood and even in school, not paying too much attention to anything else. Painting has always been an innate way of expression for him. At twenty, during College, he officially started taking drawing classes with a Hungarian artist living in Cuba - applying straight oil techniques (impasto).

Eaton's (1986) medium: varnished egg tempera dimensions 153 cm x 107 cm

HARRY TANNER

Harry Tanner was born on a sugar plantation in Cuba on the eastern part of the island where his father was working closeby for a Canadian bank, the sugarmill being the only place with medical facilities. This also explains the frequent recurrences of his Afro-Cuban topics. These convey complex ideas by using things people are familiar with, for otherwise they wouldn't be able to grasp the hidden symbolism and couldn't identify. Harry projects his ideas to people, telling us: "Look at it, think about it and relate!"

Since I was intrigued by his work, SIKAN AND TANZE, he explained the story behind it. The painting symbolizes modern woman facing traditions. 'Sikan had gone to the riverside to get some water and accidentally captured Tanze, the fish, that died on her way back to the village. When she returned, she was accused by the elders of the village and was killed - sacrificed - because of what she had done, since they believed Tanze was a magic God preserving peace among the tribes.'

This artist wants to highlight the aspects of humanity in their different facets. He is concerned, foremost, with the idea and not the use of the work of art afterwards. To him, every one of his paintings is a favourite work. Yet he does not mind parting with them. Rather he feels for the people who spend their hard-earned money to acquire them.

Harry is truly the product of the influence of several cultures, having lived in France, Cuba, Canada, and the States - continually travelling back and forth. In many ways, he sees himself as a Caribbean artist. While in Europe he studied with Andre LHOTE in Paris, a member of the Cubist School, painting mostly in oil in those days. Lhote taught Harry how to gain an analytical approach towards criticizing one's own work.

For many years he studied, in depth, the techniques of the Masters of the 16th and 17th Centuries. By experimenting, he acquired the basic technology they used. This holds true, not only of the way of applying the oil but also successive coats of it, and

In this work "Self-Portrait in Toronto," 1985, the storm is indicated by swirls - the discontinued invisible lines of the swirls being in strict adherence to the ancient law of Greek composition. medium: varnished egg tempera dimensions: 102 x 45 cm

HARRY TANNER

Tanner also does socio-historical paintings, such as the full-size portrait of Poundmaker, a Canadian hero, a Cree Blackfoot Indian who - during the Louis Riel uprising - fought the white men and won. Medium: varnished egg tempera dimension 214 x 102 cm

the way of viewing the subject. As to colours, Harry uses only three, namely blue, yellow and red - pure pigments - in conjunction with black and white. He applies many coats - often 20 to 30- combining layers of egg-tempera emulsion and oil varnish, thereby creating a most varied spectrum of colours.

In order to ensure the permanence of his colours, he uses pure pigments, processes his own oils and grinds his own colours.

For some time he was fascinated with Realist art, asking himself who were the leaders in dramatic rendition, durability of colours and ease of handling. It was then that he turned his attention to Renaissance art for many years.

This artist is committed to social issues in a humanitarian way, eager to bring about betterment and hoping to sensitize people to things they don't know. "I work my themes out over a lengthy period of time. I don't jump to do a painting right away. No. I think about it first and if, after a while, it still seems to me to be worthwhile doing, then I venture. I actually see the work of art in its entirety and only focus on details as time progresses. I first do the drawing, next the shading and then the colouring. Having played around with the overall composition, I gradually and carefully work out every single millimetre. And I always have several ideas in my head and execute several works simultaneously. It would be impossible to do all things at the same time although in the end it's all mixed up on canvas."

He added with a smile, "Besides, I have to wait for the varnish to dry."

"Do you ever encounter any dry spells?"

"Only due to economic pressure. That meant, in the past, that I had to work at something else for a while. However, since 1971 I have fully dedicated myself to painting, irrespective of financial setbacks. Luckily, there are my mother and my wife - both the sources of my continual encouragement

HARRY TANNER

photo by Misha Roberts

Babalaos (1986) medium: varnished egg tempera dimensions: 102 x 127 cm

and help in actual terms - the two dominant guiding lights in my life - complemented by the moral support of so many, many good friends."

His most recent exhibition: 12-year retrospective exhibition of Canadian-Cuban themes painted in varnished egg tempera shown at the Norman Bethune College Art Gallery, York University, February - March 1987.

Sikan and Tanze (1986) medium: varnished egg tempera dimensions: 81 x 56 cm

ALEX TAVARES

photo by Mark Sherman - 1985

Meet Alex TAVARES - painter, sculptor, printmaker, poet, and art instructor. He is a timeless universalist whose artwork - although rooted in African, East Indian, European, and North American traditions, transcends any clear cut conventional definition and challenges the viewer to perceptions of his own.

Alex, who was born on April 9th, 1934, in Zanzibar (now Tanzania), Africa, spent his childhood in Goa. Even when painting later on in Africa, the Goan seashore and the configurations his artistic eye perceived in the clouds and waves there, remained indelibly imprinted on his mind and find expression in his art. He then studied for four years, on a scholarship, in southern India at the School of Art, Madras, with emphasis on painting and sculpture.

Yet strangely enough, Alex had never thought of becoming an artist. This new direction in his life suddenly crystallized when he was 16 years old and was attending college. He frequently visited the art department by night and examined the artpieces on display. He was drawn to the Art Programme, took the test in drawing and was accepted. There, he majored first in sculpture and later in painting. He was then awarded a scholarship to pursue advanced studies at the Escuelas Profesionales and Academia de Bellas Artes in Barcelona, focussing on painting and sculpture. His calibre was such that he earned a Sculpture Award and was given a travel grant to visit the art centres in Italy.

In 1961, he returned from Spain to Goa. Here the last Portuguese Governor General, Vassal e Silva, opened Tavares' first one-man exhibition and Alex also won a Book Cover Design Award conferred by the Goan government. In 1963, he settled in Kenya where many of his paintings show a tremendous brilliance of colour and monumentally colossal proportions. These paintings offer a chromatic experience of an almost tribal sensuousness and somewhat of a pagan spirituality, if one may say so. There he held several one-man exhibitions and represented Kenya on a world-wide basis. He also won the award for a Mast Design, "Kenya Independence Street Decoration." In 1969 he then immigrated to Saskatchewan, Canada, where he had his first North American exhibition at the Art Gallery, Regina Public Library. He later moved to Toronto, making Canada his permanent home.

Alex is an extremely inspired and prolific artist. His art is never preplanned but flows freely from his subconscious and, with the exception of sculpture, is completed fairly quickly since he is driven by the creative spark of inspiration. Nor does Alex add any subsequent touch-up or finishing strokes once the

ALEX TAVARES

photo by Keith Robb

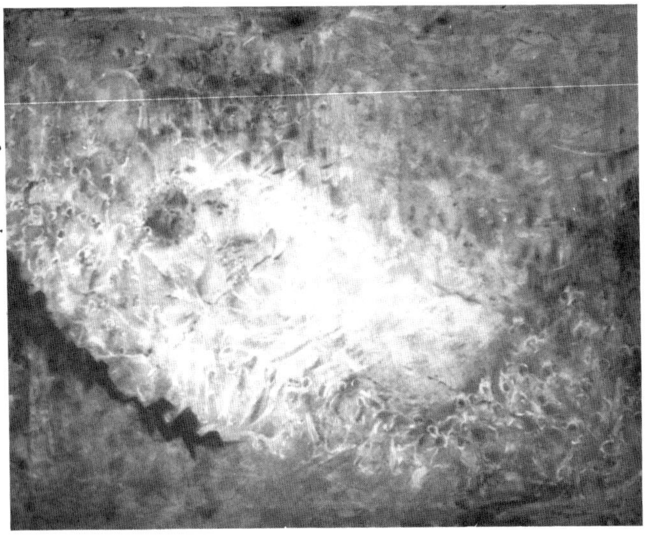

Homage To My Mother 1984 medium: acrylic painting dimensions: 66 x 52 ins. done in layers - image superimposed upon image - with lots of little figures symbolizing procession moving heavenward.

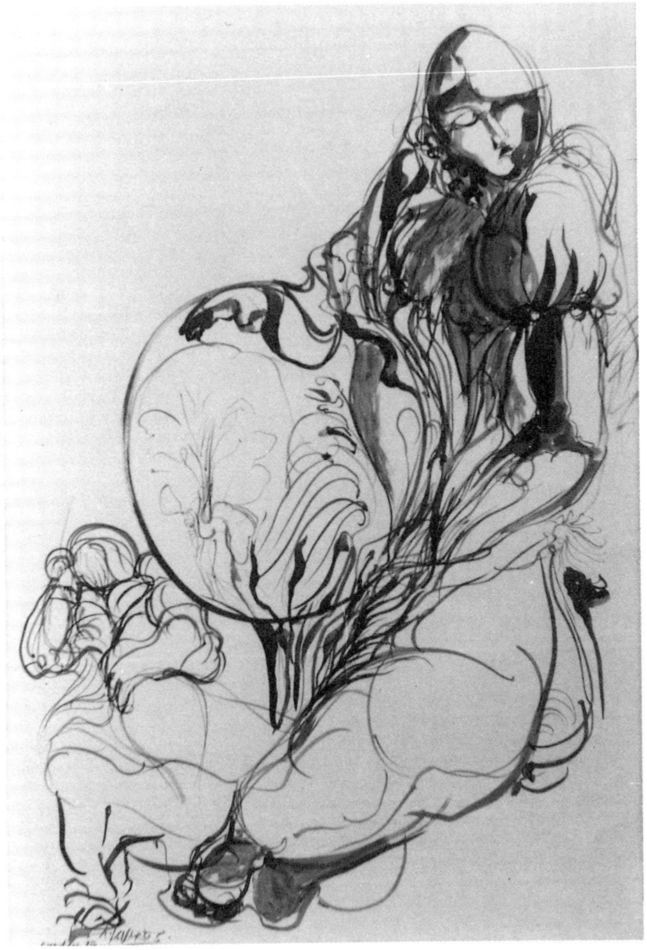

Draped Figure - Reflecting On A Reflection 1985 medium: india ink (and wash) drawing on paper dimensions: 25 x 38 ins. highlighting reflection of distant images - focussing them right in front of our eyes - depicting the phenomenon of a fleeting glance (without even the remotest intention of concentration or detailed intake) yet triggering, all of a sudden, almost total recall.

painting is completed. This artist never uses models but paints from details stored in his memory, for visual images remain permanently in his mind.

One the other hand, sculpture does take him much longer. Alex carves predominantly in wood. Some work is done in mahogany; podo - East African wood; some in Canadian oak and, the latest, in white pine. He also works in stone and metal - having done quite some experimenting lately in steel.

His more recent sculptures represent generally large monolithic figures, with the exception of Christ, whose limbs are painstakingly joined. The huge sculptures, done in Goa, served mainly to decorate the facades of new buildings or to crown the portals of churches and cathedrals.

On his flight over from the United Kingdom to Canada, Alex got many ideas for sculptures. Looking down through his window, he saw most amazing heads in the snow-like clouds. They created an effect he captured in some of his paintings. These have an almost tapestry-like semblance of a softly blending texture at a first glance. However, on closer inspection they reveal a sea of heads, done in an intriguing miniature style, which is not immediately visible to the eye until it is used to the subtly superimposed detail.

Some of his paintings belonging to that group, have the dewy mysterious quality of the serene, delicately harmonious Indian cave paintings but it always takes the eye some time to zero in on the detail.

As to his figure drawings, they show a tremendous fluidity, with such strong movement, one feels irresistibly drawn into the artwork, swept off one's feet and transported onto another plane. They are of heroic size, of monumental solidity, charged with a spiritual intensity that permeates the entire composition. His figures are most generous in their proportions and their well-rounded contours remind us of the Flemish Masters.

Alex gives new emphasis to the human figure, and despite these super dimensions, his paintings show a compact oneness of spatial composition with absolutely no loose ends. Besides, Alex quite frequently softens his strong lines by creating a certain facial vulnerability by means of superimposed white lines.

During the Sixties, Alex' work was mostly surrealistic. He did not want to add to the already existing vast stock of conventional drawings, so he created new images instead. Bewildering and disturbing drawings and paintings jump out of their canvas and - in their intensity - confront us head-on by venturing into the unfamiliar, bizarre, irrational and even grotesque at times.

These works of art, featuring quite a few figures in fragmented, disjointed and dismembered versions, yet perfectly joined and coherent in the artist's view, are pregnant with meaning. They are emotionally laden with an appeal to protect our

Weeping Mandowi River 1967 medium: acrylic dimensions: 9 x 5 ft. painting making a political statement The passive wounded woman - nostalgic for Goa - is crying for her homeland's independence, filling the river with her tears.

ALEX TAVARES

fragile human existence and are intellectually deeply stirring. These works are by no means meant to please. Rather they sensitize the viewer to a given reality - representing a prophetic warning, an explicit exhortation to protect our environment before it is too late for any kind of life to flourish.

However, the artist's ecological concerns and other man-created problems manifest themselves not only in Alex' paintings but also in his poetry. The poem, UNFURL UNFURL THE BANNERS OF CELEBRATION, served as foundation for the 'DRAPE SERIES' Alex started in 1972, each line of the poem being the title of a painting.

unfurl unfurl the banners of celebration
and pour incense in forms of clouds
in forms of pleasing foam
in forms of velvet touch
in forms of dancing boughs
softer than snow
liquid to the warm hand softer than cotton
tickling the ostrich for her feathers
and fearing not its mighty legs
so no stroke of whip may swell of wound
the damaged flesh and weep of agony
the praying desire may be grant
by squeezing only breaths of silence
into the ocean of surplus air
that clouds may descend to play
and trees may swirl in gay
children drilling round a pool
with voices that are weaving drapes
with the clean pure dew
and the birds are fluting clues of spring
calling all to unfurl their banners of celebration.

Not too long ago, Alex also studied lithography at the OCA, Ontario College of Art, under Cassidy and did five different editions of twenty prints.

In June 1986, his Show entitled "Twenty-five Year Retrospective," was held at the Art Centre in Scarborough. It featured 237 sculptures, paintings, drawings, and prints.

In 1988, Alex participated in an Exhibition at the Skylight Gallery and, in 1989, his work was represented in several group shows such as at the Mississauga Civic Centre Art Gallery, the GOA-international convention at the Toronto Harbourfront and the juried show held by the Colour & Form Society at the Campbell House Gallery in Georgetown.

Aftermath Of Ideas 1957 medium: acrylic dimensions: 35 x 60 ins. A take-off of the Inquisition (inspired by the artist's visit to Salamanca, Spain). Powerful figure drawing revealing clearly the influence of the artist's early training in sculpture. The tall figures in a tent with elongated heads and the bishop with mitre are imaginary replica of that period whereas the concrete building with the broken tower and the cart marked MAIL stand for the present-day reality - devoid of Inquisitions - but with the same type of fierce persecution existing under other names and other methods.

Besides, Alex also won last year's Consumer Gas Award of the Scarborough Arts Consilium Show juried by Doris McCarthy. For that Show, 216 works of art were submitted out of which merely 37 were selected. Alex had entered two paintings in this Show and won the award for the Drape Series painting OZONE MEMO No. 1.

He also had another One-Man Show near Parry Sound that was held simultaneously with the Parry Sound International Music Festival in August.

So far, Alex TAVARES has had seventeen One-Man Shows and he has participated in approx. fifty group exhibitions spanning four continents and covering twelve countries. His work is eagerly collected by institutions and private individuals alike.

INGA VON BOETTICHER

Meet Inga VON BOETTICHER, exponent par excellence of Alpine (Bavarian) folk art with a particular interest in the healing effect of colours.

acrylics on 1 in. pine, natural background, antiqued dimensions: height 36 cm base 25 cm

It all started with an intricately decorated trousseau chest in her grandmother's house to which Inga felt magically drawn from the time she first set her eyes on it. It also stirred a special awareness in Inga, who had been drawing and doing crafts since her early childhood. She had inclinations and talents that were further developed at the Waldorf School she attended (with special emphasis on the arts).

Then, for many years, she was very busy raising a family but was always doing some research on the side by going to libraries and museums. Initially, she would buy some existing patterns in order to thoroughly familiarize herself with the conservative styles of folk art which grew out of the farmers' firmly established customs and fairly constant lifestyle. This art was originally meant to enliven modest houses with colour, symbolism playing a major role. Consequently, typical patterns did evolve. The designs are very colourful and there is a certain purpose-orientation to this type of art. The most common objects adorned with Bavarian art are signs, plates, boxes, clocks, cradles, chests, cupboards, wardrobes, etc. Usually, the parents would give the bridal couple such a wardrobe complemented with their names, the date of marriage and - generally - a verse from the Bible.

Inga willingly explains to me the colour scheme and colours that must invariably be present in this

INGA VON BOETTICHER

acrylics on 1 in. pine, natural finish panels, on display in the Cafe Edelweiss, Etobicoke, dimensions: 72 x 50 cms

type of art, namely the basic colours: yellow, red, green and blue.

Back in the olden days, the colour lilac was reserved exclusively for ecclesiastic art.

A red rose stands for love and Jesus; three red roses symbolize the Holy Trinity; Tulips - always depicted with three little yellow tongues on top - stand for the Holy Spirit; Carnations are equated with the nails of the cross; Daisies are considered as white stars, and a star always means a new beginning.

Besides, most pieces of folk art feature a heart, vessel, vase, or cornucopia being interpreted as containing the water of life out of which everything evolves.

A bird, for instance, is a sign of protection - protecting you and your belongings. That also explains why the bird motif is so frequently found on top of the front door and on top of jewellery boxes. If a young man wanted to express his feelings of love and protection to the lady he was courting, he would present her with an item showing two birds and no further explanation was needed.

Folk art or painting on wood was the farmers' answer to wood inlay (intarsia) which city people and people of means could afford. Those costly and beautiful pieces brightened their plain and often bleak environment. Consequently, rural people started painting designs on furniture towards the end of the 16th Century. The initial designs were mainly symbols of religious or mystical significance but - as time went on - the work evolved into floral compositions

INGA VON BOETTICHER

traditional Welcome panel acrylic paints on 1 in. pine dimensions: 31 x 28 cm

decorative tree stump segment acrylics on 1 in. oak dimensions: height 85 cm base 37 cm

with some human and animal figures, though birds predominated.

Gradually the designs also became more complex. There was a design shifting from the symmetrical (ornate) to the asymmetrical (natural). In general, folk art is divided into two major stages: Baroque - 1650 to 1750 AD and Rococo - 1750 to 1850 AD.

So, at the very conventional level, folk artists are dedicating themselves to a rediscovered 17th Century art form to paint on small items and wood furniture, to which a "natural" or "antique" finish is subsequently added.

With time, folk art spread from the Alpine regions to other parts of Europe. Each country developed its own particular folk art so that we have a great variety of individual styles.

In Germany (Bavaria), Austria, and Switzerland folk art is known as "Bauernmalerei"; in Norway, as "Rosemaling"; in Holland, as "Amalande"; in France, as "Chinoiserie", and in America, as "Tolepainting".

For the past 12 years, Inga has been actively involved in Bavarian folk art and, totally so, for the past six years when people started showing special interest in her work and were eager to learn. In the beginning, she would give some patterns to her students for support or guidance but after that, eve-

INGA VON BOETTICHER

rything had to be drawn freehand. She stresses willingness to learn the "Comma"-technique, and even more willingness to practise a great deal. All work is done exclusively in acrylics.

Initially, she held special studio classes but, as demand grew, she went out to schools and for the past four years has been teaching in the Beaches area in Toronto. By special request she has held several workshops. These workshops are particularly popular since students work on one designated item such as a sign, box, etc. with something being offered for everybody from the beginner's to the advanced level. Besides, the student goes home with a finished piece of work.

Inga taught calligraphy as a visiting artist with the Toronto Board of Education in 1983/84. Since then she has been teaching calligraphy and folk art throughout Metropolitan Toronto with the Toronto Board of Education and Parks & Recreation, also holding studio classes at home.

This artist, who faithfully returns to Germany every year to do research, is enriching this art by the special relationship she has with colours. She believes that colours emit energy and vibrations and that we need colours on a subconscious level. She tries to convey a total balance of the colour-healing effect, passing it on to the people and teaching it to them.

Inga feels that since mankind nowadays is more evolved than during previous stages, we are surrounded by brighter colours and colours with faster vibrations. Yet we all need a colour balance. Hopefully this special infusion of hers into folk art will prove beneficial to all practitioners and beholders alike.

Lid of dower chest acrylics on 1" oak, antiqued dimensions: 97 cm x 51 cm

PETER ZOUDIS

Meet Panagiotis (Peter) ZOUDIS, innovative metal artist par excellence constantly exploring new concepts and ideas and forever experimenting with new techniques.

This talented artist was born in August 1952 in Kavala, Greece. He started to sketch at the age of ten and has been dreaming of being an artist ever since he can remember. During his early years, his maternal uncle, who is only slightly older than Peter, exerted great influence on him. They worked on still-lifes together and competed between themselves as to who could do a better sketch.

While he was still attending the fifth year high school course, he asked his mother for some money allowing him to go to Athens to take the examination for admission to the School of Fine Arts. In those days, you did not have to complete high school prior to acceptance but talent was the single, most important criterion. However, unfortunately, Peter did not make it this time and it hurt him so much that he could physically sense the pain of having been turned down. But the saying, "When

Parthenon medium: copper and silver dimensions: 24 x 43 ins.

PETER ZOUDIS

the going gets tough, the tough get going" holds true in Peter's case. He now worked day and night on his artwork, driven by the burning desire to be admitted to this school.

He took lessons with the ABC Correspondence Studies Institute in Athens for one year and, at the same time, also attended high school under Professor Kristos PAVLIDIS, a highly and widely respected sculptor, painter, and builder of war memorials; a professor of art whose exhibitions in many parts of the world were sponsored by various government organizations. This professor invited him to participate in painting stage settings. That proved to be the highlight of Peter's study period because he worked exclusively for and with the professor for approximately three years, and for a couple of months he was exempted from all other school work.

During the sixth year at the high school ATHONIADA, under the auspices of the Orthodox Church, he studied iconography under Professor Ioannis MONAHOS and graduated with top marks.

As soon as he finished high school during the next summer he took off to Athens and tried for one of the schools affiliated with the School of Fine Arts. He attended preparatory classes with Professor Ioanna OIKONOMIDOU from the early morning hours through the stifling heat of the day till darkness set in, working with models. These schools provide special courses in still-life, life drawing, charcoal sketching, etc. - and he was among the 65 candidates chosen out of a total of 4000 hopeful applicants.

The introductory year prepares the students for specialties such as painting, engraving and sculpture. Peter was extremely interested in sculpting but could see that was not his specialty after all. Rather than having an opportunity to sit for one supplemental examination, he would now have to start all over again.

It so happened that at that particular moment he learned about the German Academy HÖHERE LEHRANSTALT - deutsches Lehr-system für Gebrauchs - und Werbegrafik (applied advertising and commercial art) where he enrolled in a highly demanding course involving a three-year programme.

At the Academy he worked really hard, full-heartedly enjoying himself, and he passed with flying

Athena medium: copper and silver dimensions: 24 x 36 ins.

colours. On top of his studies in arts, he was even granted a government scholarship to study the German language for one year in Munich, and it was upon completion of that course that Panagiotis came to Canada in 1976.

Peter liked Canada so much that he decided to stay. He taught academic subjects at a Greek community school, at a Catholic school for 1-1/2 years and at a school at Old Shepherd and Pauline Street.

Then, one day, totally out of the blue, he ran into a Greek friend who lived in Montreal. The friend had just brought a professional metal artist from Europe, and the two had opened a joint-venture business for decorative items. However, after a couple of months the friend of Peter's and his partner split and left over was an entire coil of copper. They didn't know what to do with it. He approached Peter. "You are an artist. Maybe you want to work with it. Maybe you could buy it from us?"

No sooner said than done and what a surprise! Peter became so fascinated with metal arts and got so wrapped up in the work that a tremendously powerful energy drove him. Believe it or not - he seemed to have a special knack and acquired such skills that the friend, who was actually supposed to teach Peter, was deeply impressed with his creations and his amazing reliefs and now came to Peter for guidance.

Soon, during Caravan week, he had his first Show in the Greek community and it turned out to be a big success - almost a total sell-out. This gave him a real boost, since he hadn't quite expected it.

Reminiscing about the time when he was still teaching, he admits he appreciated that extra income since it gave him the badly needed artistic independence to experiment and perfect techniques. It was rather crucial in terms of freedom and artistic honesty, for he did not have to sacrifice on quality for lack of funds. Besides, he has never been intimidated at the thought of making mistakes because he feels the resulting learning experience to be a valuable lesson.

Pegasus "painting" medium: copper dimensions: 24 x 43 ins.

Natural Forces medium: brass and silver dimensions: 24 x 43 ins.

He still has that artistic innocence of following his inspiration. Even when commissioned to do certain pieces, he never serializes but tries to visualize the artwork in relation to its future beholder and the environment in which it will find a home.

Next, Peter opened an art studio at Gerrard and Greenwood. He also exhibited, for three years in a row, at the Canadian National Exhibition. In 1979, he won the Achievement Award in Arts, Crafts, and Hobbies as a copper artist, and his art really won recognition. That feedback from the public did add impetus!

Peter smilingly points out that whereas people can make mistakes when working with sheet metal, for instance, there is no second chance with metal because it shows. Consequently, his work has to be right the first time. There are no shortcuts and there is no patching-up!

Peter learned from his CNE exhibition experience that the most expensive artwork was bought by people from the States. He now participates in US-based Shows such as the Allentown Festival in Buffalo involving close to five hundred artists. Once again - he experienced a smashing success. A total sell-out! It is important for him to have clients who are genuinely happy with their art acquisition.

Since 1980 he hasn't had many shows in Canada but he has usually nine to ten exhibitions per year in the States, and he is, indeed, very satisfied with the results from those shows and pleased to have clients come back for more artwork.

One day, the President of the Greek community, Dr. Leonides POLIMENAKOS, who was familiar with Peter's work, approached him wondering whether he could do an iconostasis in metal. "Quite an unusual concept," he commented, "But certainly worth a try." Of course, the matter of whether to do the iconostasis in metal or wood had been brought to the attention of the Greek Council. An overwhelming 28 members voted in favour of metal. So Peter got the commission and was overjoyed.

PETER ZOUDIS

Two Dancers medium: brass and silver dimensions: 24 x 36 ins.

Feverishly he drew designs. He was now working with dimensions covering 45 feet in length and 12 feet in height and it took him a year and a half to complete these. He worked to his heart's content - appreciating this unique opportunity to show what he could do - his inspiration taking flights of fancy. Then, followed a commission for a synagogue door, decorative panels for several restaurants, etc.

How does he get the ideas for his work? At time, he draws on mythology, at other times he indulges himself in motifs such as ships and waves, animals, then again he illustrates daily life occurrences, abundantly curvaceous females in motion, and abstracts. His brain is constantly teeming with ideas and he is always thinking of new working methods. Sticking to the same techniques would be far too boring for him. Peter needs the challenge of innovation, thrives on it so-to-speak. Yet despite his undeniable ingenuity, he is touchingly humble, realizing fully well that there is always a new avenue to explore, different concepts to experiment with - always something new to learn. He is presently working in brass, aluminum and enamels.

How long does a "metal painting" usually take him to execute? It might take anywhere from one week to two months, depending on the detail and the intricacy of the artwork involved as well as its overall dimensions.

Lately, he further diversified - adding ornamental tiles to his specialty. With these enamelled tiles, Peter controls the entire process in order to guarantee the freshness of any specific colour required and their shades. Although these are more series-oriented and commercial, they allow him to continue his other highly artistic work while still providing for the necessities of life.

Taking one last look at all the impressive "metal paintings", I ask the artist - while admiring his desk covered in ornamental copper panelling - what his dreams for the future might be all about.

"I want to do substantially more artwork and have greater exposure in art galleries all over Canada and the United States."

Peter's work is represented in many private collections in Greece, the Federal Republic of Germany, Japan, Australia, Canada, and most areas of the United States.

35556
709.71 DEY
Dey-Bergmoser, Olga, 1938-
More faces, more spaces : artists in Canada